HEALING

HEALING

David Elliott

Hawk
Press

Healing
By David Elliott

Published by:
Hawk Press
4510 Alumni Avenue
Los Angeles, CA 90041
http://www.thereluctanthealer.com/
(323)908-6058

Names have been changed to protect the identity of private parties.

Book Cover Design by Charlie Griak
Illustrations by Charlie Griak
Diagrams by Charlie Griak
Edited by Corrie Borris, Katrina Rivers, Gali Kronenberg

Publisher's Cataloging-in-Publication
(Provided by Quality Books, Inc.)

Elliott David, 1958-
Healing / David Elliott.
p. cm.
Includes index.
LCCN 2009935363
ISBN-13: 978-0-9753910-6-8
ISBN-10: 0-9753910-6-2

Spiritual healing and spiritualism.
  Self-actualization (Psychology)—Religious aspects.
  Title.

        BF1275.F3E45 2009   615.8'52
                QBI09-600151

"Open the Work"

Table of Contents

WRAPPING UP THE HEALING JOURNEY

ოი

LIST OF DIAGRAMS

☙❧

LIST OF EXERICES

Introduction

What if you could heal yourself of any illness, addiction, or chronic condition? How much freedom would you experience if you were not dependent on health care? How empowered would you feel if you had the keys to healing, not only on the physical level, but on emotional, mental and spiritual levels as well?

If you need healing in your life, this book is for you. However you came to this book, whether by accident, curiosity, or as a gift from a friend, no matter. I am happy to meet you!

For more than twenty years, I have been working to help people heal. My philosophy is simple. I accept a higher power; whatever name you give it—God, Creator, Spirit, Grace—I acknowledge this higher power as the greatest force in the Universe and recognize it as the unifying Power of Love; I accept that we are all connected through this source of energy to heal our lives!

In this book, I will describe how you can connect to the Universal Energy Flow that is at the heart of creation.

Learning to tap into this stream of consciousness can transform your health and bring you the love you desire.

My first book, *The Reluctant Healer*, is about my early journey in life and how all the pieces of healing came together for me. That book provides a detailed explanation of the process and tools I use as a healer when working with people in my practice. The several topics that I introduced about healing, I take much deeper. As you will discover, **healing** and **love** are at the heart of what I share with you now.

WHAT IS HEALING?

Healing is the journey back to our natural state of balance and harmony that is called love. Healing becomes necessary when you lose contact with that natural state, when there is a disturbance in the Universal Flow. Healing can take place in many ways, each as uniquely individual as you. The one constant is for you to be connected to you. As Socrates said, *"Know thyself."* When you are willing to accept responsibility for everything you create in your life, you can heal yourself.

The power to heal lies within you. If you got yourself into this mess, you innately know what you need to do to get out. My role is to remind you of that, to be witness and hold space for you to make the necessary changes in your life without judgment in a safe, supportive and loving way.

WHAT IS LOVE?

This most desired human emotion, love, is the energy of the heart and soul that brings balance, harmony, and healing. Love expands and uplifts you when felt and expressed. When you feel love you feel connected to all things through your heart. As you read on, you'll discover that self-love is the key to healing. I will show you how the absence of self-love creates disease through negativity, while the positive energy of self-love creates health and well-being.

I have noticed that the right amount of love will heal any affliction. It is not the love you can get from me or from another, it is the love you generate inside of yourself. As simple as it sounds, the antidote for anything is to love you.

HOW CAN THIS BOOK HELP YOU HEAL?

This book will take you deep into what is keeping you from thriving in all aspects of your life. To achieve healing this book requires commitment and a willingness to do the work. The best way to do this is to sit down and take your time with it. If you roll up your sleeves and do the inner work, you will heal.

As in *The Reluctant Healer*, each section has a series of practical exercises designed to build one upon the other, each facilitating the next. I will bring you face-to-face with the self-created blocks inside that are stopping you. I will guide you every step of the way and support you with your healing journey. The deeper you dig, the more gold you will discover. Each discovery will lead you further down the path to self-love and healing. If you choose to embark on this journey expect your life to blossom.

THE ROADMAP TO HEALING

I call Section One The Crucible because it lays out the material with which you can truly engage and deal with yourself. Do you love yourself or not? That is the question. I am being very black and white about this because of the importance of self-love. By working diligently with this material you will move out of any gray areas of low self-love. In the experience of self-love versus no self-love, we look at the positive ways you can connect to the Universal Energy Flow through love and exchange. Exchange is the word I use to describe the flow of energy from the Universe when we choose to love. We also look at some of the traits that can develop when self-love is lacking. If you recognize any of these traits in yourself they will identify the places where you are stuck. The exercises pinpoint these areas so you can illuminate and heal them.

Throughout the book, I reference the Love Exchange Diagram on the following page, which shows the different paths of life based on the choice we each make to love ourselves or not. The graphic illustrates how self-love spirals out of the heart leading to an exchange of love with all things. As this exchange happens it connects you to the larger Universal Energy Flow and the Grace that flows back to you from it. In the 'no self-love' portion of the diagram rooted in the second chakra with no connection to Universal Energy Flow you will see many of the negative afflictions affecting people; these are based on the negative emotions anger, fear and sadness.

In the process of healing you can always make the choice to return to love. This decision is the cornerstone of spiritual relationship with oneself. In my philosophy of us all being one, I seek to bring healing to you, and to the planet, by teaching you the importance of self-love.

Is it really so simple? Is self-love really the answer? I have asked myself this question for many years and I know that it is. Do you already know this? Do you know the areas you are stuck in life, and why? And even if you do, are you able to

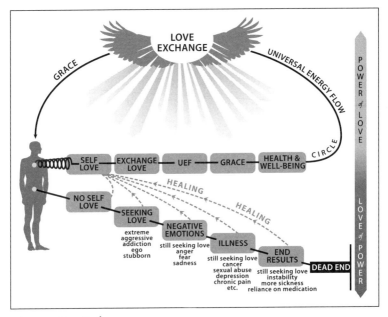

Diagram 1: Love Exchange

move past them? If not, travel along with me. I see this book as a tattered bedside companion, which has been thrown across the room more than once. Keep it with you. Work with it, study it, do the exercises and learn to love yourself. Set yourself free!

In Section Two, The Work, I introduce the ways I have developed to bring self-love, consciousness and awareness to all aspects of one's life. The information the Universe has given me to heal myself has become the technique that I use to teach and help others heal. I take the key concept of self-love from Section One and show you how to develop it into your own navigation system through the use of intuition and creativity. If you have the desire to access and trust your intuition and to risk expressing your creativity, this process is the journey and the reward!

In Section Three, we delve deeper into Personal Healing. Here we learn how to bring healing to key experiences in life where many people need it. We examine sexual abuse, cancer, marriage and divorce, intimate relationships, leadership roles, and money because these areas are consistently what bring people into my healing room. If you can receive and accept the healing message in these examples and exercises, the information will connect through your own experience and you will regain balance and harmony in your life.

Section Four, The Healing Tools, is a summation of the tools I use in the healing work, as well as some background on how I came to them. I make these as accessible as I can with lots of description and a free offering to help get you on your way. Find the nuggets!

Finally, in Section Five, we look at the transformative power of Gratitude. I talk about the people and all the various plants, animals and Beings of Light that I work with and for which I am grateful. It is a daily, moment-to-moment practice with me and it is life changing—I hope it will inspire you to find the gratitude in your life.

To summarize, I invite you one more time to do the work. Do what you can. Allow this book to penetrate your scar tissue, let it into your vulnerabilities, and into your heart. I have so much respect for those willing to work on themselves. If you are one of them, I will do my best to lend you a hand.

MORE ABOUT ME

Born and raised on a farm in Kentucky, I spent my childhood immersed in nature. By the time I was eighteen I was restless and ready to experience wider aspects of life. I knew deep inside that I had a purpose and I needed to be off the farm to find it.

Eventually, my journey brought me to Los Angeles where I decided to be an actor. At the time it was a strange choice, and I ended up realizing I wanted acting more than it wanted me. What it did teach me has proven to be priceless. I learned about myself—my energy, creativity, shyness, and spirit. I was dedicated and I focused on acting with all my being. I worked some, joined the union and called myself an actor for several years. Then even stranger things began to happen. People started to grab me on the streets telling me I was a healer. I thought they were those 'New Age crazies' from Southern California. It kept happening and finally I had to deal with what this was about.

I talk in detail about this experience in *The Reluctant Healer*, as well as in Section Four of this book. My farm upbringing growing corn and soybeans was very practical, and even though I left the farm, it took a lot for me to consider myself a healer. I was more than reluctant about it for several years, yet just as acting taught me about myself, healing took my self-awareness much deeper into the core of who I am.

What I reluctantly learned about healing began to bring answers to the questions I had been living with my whole life. Healing fulfilled my desperate appetite to know my spirit, to find resolution inside myself about my purpose in life and the reason why I am here. When I quit resisting the call of my spirit, everything opened up. Answers to my questions came flooding in. Consequently, the purpose of this book is to share them with you. This is my job.

I was raised Catholic and I always had more questions than the Church had answers. I needed to find the truth for myself. Love is the truth for me. As I mentioned before, when I speak of Universal Energy Flow, I include all the ways to which 'God' is referred. I do this to be inclusive of all religions and spiritual teachings. I see the similarities within all those that are based in love, and I support any spiritual practice that works for you. I engage with many cultures, nations and people from around the world and I choose to relate to everyone in the same way, with an open heart.

What is teaching really? I think it comes down to speaking in a way that can be heard. The art form of healing, and writing for that matter, is to be straight with people and to enable them to hear you at the same time. I do my best to do that in this book.

Some of the information you will encounter will hit you where you need it most, where you are stuck! It may seem forceful and confronting and it may irritate you. Some sections may even sound negative—the cold hard facts are not always pretty. Nevertheless, I come from a place of love at all times. Try to open your heart and let it in.

I do care about you. I encourage you to do the exercises and spend the time to get the healing you deserve. I am not writing this book for fame or money as I already attract more attention than I am comfortable with. Where I focus most of my consciousness is in my relationship with the Universe. I am writing this book because it is my purpose and commitment to share what I have learned and to help as many people as I possibly can in this lifetime. Are you ready? Let's go!

section one

THE CRUCIBLE

The Crucible

LOVE

What does it take to get you to remember the Power of Love? What does it take to get you to remember the Power of Love that resides in you? Love connects you to you. From that vantage point you are then connected to everything, everywhere. Love is.

As you see in the simple diagram on the following page there are two choices—Self-Love versus No Self-Love. Self-love is based in the heart, and no self-love is based in the lower regions of the body, centered in the pelvis. I will be expanding on this diagram throughout the book.

Love within you from the heart connects you to everything, everywhere. Without this connection to love you will be lost, continually looking outside of yourself for love to fix you. At times you may think you have found it. However, when it is based in someone or something outside of you it will always fail to complete the spiral of love, because it is a straight line between whatever is outside and you.

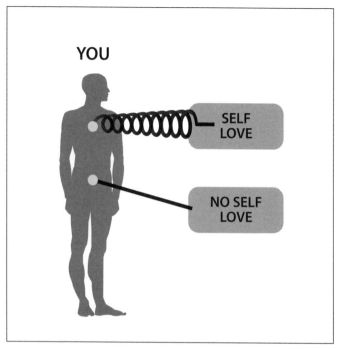

Diagram 2 – Self-Love versus No Self-Love

Love from inside you emanates from a circular center point, from the center of your heart chakra. A chakra is an Eastern philosophy term for wheel, which is an energy center of spiritual power that spins in the body. The energy of love moves in and out of the heart chakra in a spiral. When you connect to your heart, to the love inside of you, you will always remember the Power of Love. Once the heart is open it draws the essence or soul (I use these two words interchangeably) in from the Universe through the crown and the essence merges with the love in the heart.

As your essence pours into you it is felt as love. Love is the language of the soul. Together love and essence create, feed, and nurture each other as they merge in the heart. Take away love and the essence cannot grow in you, take away the essence and love cannot grow in you. Without love, without the essence, you end up with a Love Of Power, which is an ego driven, empty state of existence signified in Diagram 2 as no self-love. This empty state will always have a person seeking love from outside sources and it will be motivated by the ego as it pushes the negative emotions—anger, fear and sadness—in the second chakra.

Gary, a 55 year-old psychologist, came to me complaining of no love in his life. He felt like he was very open, loveable, and available to relationship. I told him he was not as available as he thought. He was rather offended. I explained that his openness was in his mind. I told him that I experienced him as being quite forward and aggressive with his energy, especially his sexual energy. He defended this by saying this is how gay men are. I suggested that this was a general assessment and that I knew many gay men who were not aggressive with their openness and sexuality. He persisted saying he felt like he deserved love in his life, that he had so much to offer. I agreed with him and explained the openness he felt in his mind needed to be in his heart. He argued that his heart was open. I said, "No it isn't, and that is why you are not being responded to like you wish."

There was a slight opening, and he backed up saying he had been hurt and needed to protect his heart. I said, "Fine, we have all been hurt, you can be careful with your heart. Nevertheless, you have to open your heart to love you." He starred blankly at me. I continued, "You don't love you very much, rather you are waiting to love you, and you are wait-

ing to be excited about you when someone comes into your life to love you. You are playing the waiting game!"

Gary was starting to fidget. He said, "I say this to clients all the time. Tell me something I don't know!" I said, "Now we're getting somewhere! It is not what you say, it is what you do. Are you going to love you, or not?" He said, "How?" I told him that he had to find the feeling of love inside his heart for himself, that this was what he was desperately searching for. He said, "How!" I said,

- *Start with the areas you like about yourself*
- *Encourage the areas you like to grow with gratitude*
- *Find the good*
- *Cultivate the good*
- *Be positive*
- *Grow the positive into love*
- *Become a gardener for love inside of you*

"If you do this how much better of a psychologist will you become? How much more impact will your words have?" He replied, "A lot! Are there any more specific ways I can grow my positive garden of love?" "You have to want it", I told him. "You have to choose to heal your life. If you choose it, it will happen. I guarantee it. Open your heart to the sensitive, open, loving boy you were when you were four years old." "Why four?" he asked.

"I don't know why four, that's what I heard," I said. "Four was the year my father died," he said. "I changed, I think I lost my innocence then. Was that random? Did you just say four? It is not that apparent is it? How do you hear those things?" I smiled, "It was luck I guess, but if I were you I would deal

with that little boy place inside of you. It is time he knows that life is safe, that he is safe, that he can love again." "Is it that easy?" he asked.

Gary began to sob. I smiled at the little boy. Spirit moved between us. My intuition nudged me to reach out and take his hand and look him in the eye. I said, "I promise you if you keep this place open in your heart, you will create love in your life." A hawk screamed overhead, a hummingbird darted in front of the window. Gary nodded his head in agreement. Then a crow cawed very loudly. He looked outside and said, "That's strange, my father always loved crows." I said, " Let your father into your heart right now." The room got very hot, the wind blew the curtains, he sobbed some more, and we both felt the spirit of his father present for the rest of the session. The crow kept on cawing. I joked that he and his father had a lot of catching up to do!

Ultimately Gary opened his heart that day. He healed something he had been holding onto for a long time. He had been mad at God for taking his father away. The little boy was mad and skeptical about life. He thought 'love hurts'. He reconnected to his spirit and the spirit of his father, and the end result is that he is loving himself more than before and is starting to date someone!

All healthy human aspects and dimensions of love begin inside of you. Once you trust yourself to open your heart to you, this connection to your essence becomes the most important relationship in your life! It is the only way to have a relationship with love that can grow outward through you to Universality. From there the heavens are yours! Love expressed outwardly to others is a healthy experience with clarity, boundary, exchange, giving, receiving, and freedom. It is all there to be explored because there is a foundation of security about your relationship with yourself.

> *One of the most powerful experiences of my life happened early on with the pranayama breathing meditation as I felt my heart open and love pour out of me to everyone and everything. As this was happening, I felt a tremendous amount of energy start to spiral into me through my crown. Everything was spinning! I remember saying out loud, "My essence is in my heart." My friend Tim, who was supporting me, heard me and said, "Yes, you just had a soul merge!"*

In this case it is not about the chicken or the egg. It is all about looking to yourself for the relationship you crave. Dig deeper inside of yourself. The way your essence moves into and through you I refer to as spirit. Trust yourself to feel the energy of your spirit, which I liken to the personality of your essence or soul. The particular vibration, the flow of fire and heat as energy, the goose bump movement of electricity through your nervous system are all ways that your soul, or essence, expresses itself as the spirit. As you develop this relationship with your soul and learn to love its movement and expression, then you can become one with it as you realize it contains the answers you are looking for. This relationship takes you home to all you have ever been, and ever stood for. It gives you the confidence to know who you are so you can institute boundaries to preserve and protect your essence. It is all so simple when you give in to the Power of Love within you, the memories within you, the source within you.

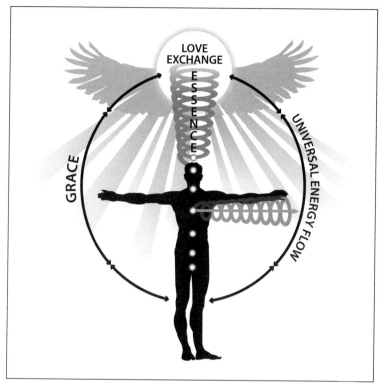

Diagram 3 - Essence 1

Love expressed from the purity of this well is eternal. It contains all the wisdom of the Universe because it is the Universe. It connects all things as a web of light flowing in all directions. The only person holding the key is you. When you find it you comprehend it is all the same energy flow—birth, life, death, love, peace, faith, and trust.

Love is as easy to receive, as it is to give. The flow never stops, even without physical form our essence is always flowing as spirit throughout the consciousness of the Universe.

LOVE — EXERCISE 1

1. Write down all the ways you love yourself. If you have difficulty doing this exercise then we have found the key to your healing! Risk Loving Yourself!

2. Work at this until it is easy and something you do everyday. It may seem cliché but it is vitally important to your healing on all levels—physically, emotionally, mentally, and spiritually.

A letter to you,

As I was riding my bike this morning I was thinking about you. Yes, you! I was thinking about the reader, the person engaged with this book, and truly all the people I have ever worked with. So many ask me daily how do I love myself? Tell me how to do it?

One person who knows I am writing this book asked me for the third time, "I'm so curious to hear about the steps you lay out so that a reader can take the journey from self-loathing to self-love."

I am thinking about this as I am pedaling up the mountain, no easy feat! I realize I am in my head thinking of how to communicate more about loving oneself. I am not connected to this moment, and I am struggling. This mountain is kicking my butt. And I look at my old bike, I expect it to get me up the mountain and back. I acknowledge this fifteen year-old lovely Specialized Stump Jumper mountain bike. I thank it for its service. I love myself in that same moment, because I have moved into a place of gratitude in my heart. It softened me.

Then I connected to my body, I felt my heart. It opened. I smiled. Love feels good!

I acknowledge myself and my discipline. I am riding every morning because I have committed to take care of my physical vessel this summer. I breathed in the clear mountain air. I received it in my lungs, my body pulsed with Universal Energy! I felt it. I loved myself, the Universe loved me, an exchange happened. I thought about you. Can I convey the simplicity of this to you?

Then I thought about the self-loathing question. It is as simple as being too caught up in oneself, and having little, or no awareness of the exchange with the Universe that happens when you love. Where do we place our attention—on the negative or the positive? Loathing does not make sense to me, why waste the time?

Back to more important things! I breathed in more air, blood pumped through my heart, and I smiled. Riding up the mountain with a big smile on my face! I felt the love, I felt the exchange, and the birds in the trees sang louder, or more accurately, I could hear them because I became attuned to their song and their love. Nature is love. I loved myself, and I acknowledged this exchange. I think about you, what if you do not connect to Nature? Does anyone not connect to Nature? Maybe someone feeling self-loathing.

I shift back to the ride and I pedal on. Amazingly the ride has become a lot easier! I am feeling my body, the blood pumping through my muscles, the air on my face, the beautiful trees, this Sandia mountain, and the birds!

I write this for you. Receive the simplicity and apply it. It works, love is a moment to moment reality, no matter where you are. It is there just as easily in the big city, as it is here in the mountains of New Mexico. I am no more suited to a spiritual life than you are. I live a spiritual existence because I choose to, and I practice. Not perfectly, but I practice, and I have discipline. When I am choosing to love, to be in the moment, and to be exchanging love, awareness, and awe with the Universe, magic happens. I know it sounds a little over the top, but it is like paradise to me!

This is why I am writing, I have to share this with as many people as I can. I am love, I am connected to my employer—the Universe, and the energy flow here is infinite.

I continue on...love is flowing, and writing is my expression.

Love, David

EXCHANGE

The positive approach to the bigger picture revolves around love and exchange. They work hand in hand and I hope you have done the prior exercise, and you are loving you as we move on into understanding exchange. See Diagram 4 and you will notice with self-love there will be an exchange of love; with no self-love you will be seeking love.

Here's how I define and use the terms in this section, see if you can apply them to your life.

Love – An energy of the heart and soul. It expands and uplifts you when felt and expressed. It is the human emotion people most desire. When you feel love within, it spirals outward and connects you to all existence through the opening of the heart.

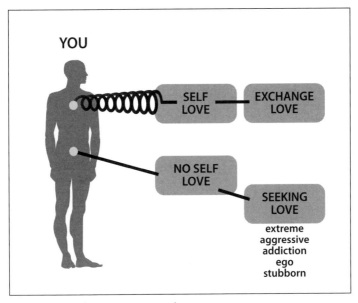

Diagram 4 - Exchange Love versus Seeking Love

Exchange – The flow of energy or consciousness given and received as energy, respect, value, appreciation, and love. It can also refer to goods, services and money.

Universal Energy Flow – The natural flow of energy exemplified in the earth, sun, moon, sky, stars, waterfalls, oceans, rivers, springs, deserts, glaciers, air, wind, storms, forests, trees, jungles, wildlife, and rainbows. Humans can access the Universal Energy Flow when they are in a place of love. It can flow into them and be exchanged with.

Continuing on, I explain how all of the stages build on each other in Diagram 5. Self-love creates a positive energetic exchange with others and enables you to connect with the Universal Energy Flow. No self-love creates seeking love externally, which in turn sets you up for many negative experiences and negative behaviors such as being extreme, aggressive, addicted, ego driven, and stubborn. These behaviors become the catalyst for the negative emotions of anger, fear and sadness. Try to stay with the simplicity of the diagram. I will talk in detail about each behavior in the sections to follow.

When I say 'exchange', some people think I am primarily referring to physical goods, services and money, and even though these can be one aspect of exchange, I am more interested in what happens in the spiritual flow with love and exchange. I am interested in how things open for people. How do you get energy moving when you are stuck? How do you get things flowing?

If you can cultivate self-love, you will create relationship with everything around you, which will bring the spiritual

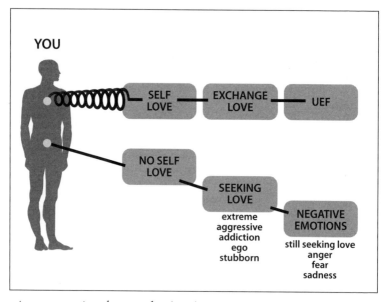

Diagram 5 – Universal Energy Flow (UEF) versus Negative Emotions

aspect of exchange into your consciousness. When you understand this concept it will be the foundation that will set you free. If there is any place, relationship, or thing where you feel under-appreciated or stuck, then your approach to exchange within yourself is off, and you will need to go back and find the place where you are not loving you. As I am using the word exchange, see what ideas come to you about what I am referring to.

EXCHANGE ~ EXERCISE 2

Do this exercise before reading any further in the book.

1. Write down your definition for exchange.

2. Write down every relationship where you do not feel appreciated and valued in your life.

3. Write down the areas where you feel abundantly appreciated and valued.

4. Compare the two—appreciated to unappreciated.

5. Check in with yourself right now, do you live in deficit around exchange? Or do you live with abundance? How do you feel in this moment—uplifted, or deflated? Your feeling will tell you where you stand with exchange.

If you feel deficit, deflated, or heavy around this exercise with exchange take the following actions. These are the places you are stuck! Take your time with this whole exercise, no need to rush, even if uncomfortable stuff is coming up. Let's deal with it now; as we strengthen your relationship to love and exchange, you will heal.

- Forgive those who take from or walk all over you. They are your biggest teachers. Take your power back from them and lovingly set them free. Let them go by releasing your neediness for their love. Love yourself instead!

- Go back and read aloud the ways you love yourself from the prior section. Do this until you feel the vibration of love.

- Develop the discipline to fill yourself up with love. Give to yourself and exchange love with you; until you can do this you will always create takers, abusers, and con artists to teach you about self-love and self-esteem. Be your own teacher!

People have asked me have I always felt self-love. Have I always loved myself? I tell them most of the time I have but it has not always been 100%. I have wavered and my biggest lessons were with my father and issues of control and anger. We were quite combative when I was a teenager and at times neither of us felt appreciated by the other. Nevertheless, deep down we knew there was much love between us. We finally decided we were a lot alike and created an alliance that carried us more peacefully down the road. Through it all I never lost respect for myself, or my father, and ultimately I learned that I had to love and approve of myself. If I was happy and content, most of the time my dad and I got along fine. I began to realize this was true in most of my relationships.

As you learn to love and give to yourself, the Universe simultaneously opens a flow of energy that expands your vibration of self-love. This builds as you consciously exchange with the Universe. You exchange with the Universal Energy Flow by taking the time to acknowledge it, love it, and trust it (e.g. learn, teach, or write about it). As you trust the unconditional love flowing through you it expands towards others, and flows back to the Universe, which immediately sends the flow back to you in the form of grace. It is one big circle.

Grace - The Universal Energy Flow as it flows back to us in a form we can recognize such as a vibration, temperature, or tone of energy. This description is slightly different from the religious context. In this context, grace is the byproduct created from the agreement to love and exchange.

In Diagram 6 you will see Grace versus Illness depicted. If you can get the underlying principles you will start to understand the spiritual basis for all illness, affliction, and negative traits affecting people.

The blessings from the Universal Energy Flow that come back to you in the form of grace result in feelings of abundance, inspiration, enthusiasm, excitement and, most importantly, self-love. This flow of energy when accessed and used by humans is the fountain of youth, the wellspring to existence, and it saves the body from having to use up its personal energy supply, which is finite. The Universal Energy Flow is **infinite** and is a natural resource that exists beyond human realms and is not controlled by humans. It has an ability to give us tremendous amounts of energy if tapped into, which happens by exchanging with it. Accessing the Universal Energy Flow is the key to success, because it gives

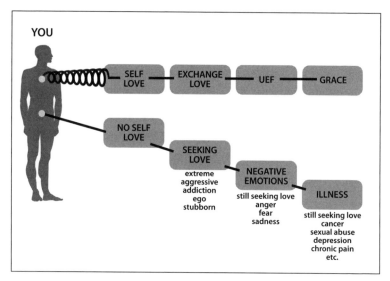

Diagram 6 – Grace versus Illness

you life force. Have you felt this before? Abundance, inspiration, enthusiasm, excitement, and self-love?

> *I am writing this book in the summer monsoon season in the mountains of New Mexico. There have been some wonderful rainstorms and beautiful rainbows happening almost daily. Every time it rains I stop what I am doing to acknowledge the moisture, clouds, lightning, thunder, and the sound, smell, and feel of the rain. The Universal Energy Flow during these storms is enlivening and powerful. I breathe it in and walk in the rain. Oftentimes a rainbow emerges and I humble myself to the display of beauty and light; light dancing in the sky!*
>
> *I cannot affect this rainbow. It is going to happen with or without me; however, the way I choose to engage with it can affect me! I approach the rainbow with my consciousness. I humbly and respectfully ask it for a blessing. The blessing is*

palpable. I can feel the energy from the rainbow and the rain giving me life force. I humbly and respectfully ask the rainbow to bless my writing and to help me get these points across. I tell the rainbow of the challenges I am facing describing its Universal properties and the way it can be engaged with for healing and for Universal Energy Flow. I humbly ask it to shine all of its colors of illumination on my computer, and this material, and for it to carry through to the finished book. I humbly do this for you!

As I finish this simple but 100% conscious process, I feel a Universal flow of energy move into me. It tickles and touches me, my heart warms, opens wider and I feel the grace from the Universe; the personality of the Universe in that moment. A hummingbird dances over my head and the rainbow shines even brighter.

As grace flows into us we live in harmony and have abundant energy to love the self more; the Power of Love multiplies. Love vibrates at a balanced frequency, which the Universe recognizes, and love harmonizes everything it flows to and through. Love connects us into the huge natural Universal Energy Flow, when this happens grace flows back to us, or simply the larger flow of energy fills us up!

Grace is in spiritual form as energy, and even better it is in spiritual form as Universal Energy Flow. Having awareness of love, exchange, Universal Energy Flow, and grace creates health and well-being, which teaches us the aspects of life where human ego and intellect are not limiting factors because the heart is open. Whereas when the heart is not open a negative path of imbalance, illness and disease take

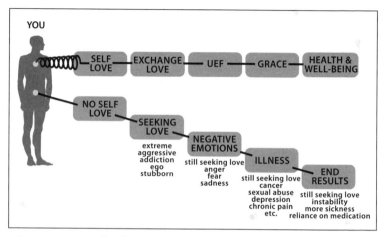

Diagram 7 – Love and Exchange versus Negative End Results

hold. The positive path of consciousness brings us to a place of harmony, peace, and contentment. It completes us, and it happens in an empowering self-fulfilling way that opens us to the beauty of nature, which is Universal Energy Flow at its best!

> *Recently an injured hawk showed up at a friend's house and knowing I had experience with wild animals my friend asked me if I could help (It is always wise to contact your local animal services when you encounter an injured wild animal). As I was making the arrangements to get the hawk to the wildlife shelter, I formed a bond with him. We enjoyed each other's company and had a mutual respect for each other. Every time I was around this creature I experienced a tremendous amount of love, exchange, and Universal Energy Flow, and when I dropped him off at the facility the worker said it looked like he was well taken care of. I immediately felt Grace flow into my body when I heard those words. The experience*

brought me face-to-face with the commitment I made to help rescue hawks, owls, hummingbirds, and other animals as part of the Creative Healing Arts Center nonprofit organization, which I am in the process of getting finalized. I am doing this because it is something I have been guided to do for a long time. I talk about this organization more on p. 235.

If you talk to the animals, they will talk to you and you will know each other. If you do not talk to them, you will not know them. And what you do not know, you will fear. What one fears one destroys. –Chief Dan George

Dig deeply into the questions in Exercise 3 and pay attention to what comes up. This exercise will outline how to

preserve your life force, and it will show you how to exchange beyond your ego, mind, and limiting self-beliefs. When you realize this, many of your worries and dramas will disappear. When you are willing to get out of the way and let something bigger than you through, the Universe becomes your employer, and what an equal opportunity employer it is! When you say, "Yes!" and step into spiritual relationship with the Universe, everything makes sense. For example, writing a book:

- You have an intuition about writing

- Feel energy (tingly sensations) as you are having the intuition

- Think about what just came to you, maybe you saw the book cover

- Remember people telling you that you should write

- Get goose bumps (the vibration gets stronger)

- Start to write the book

- People ask you if you are writing a book

- Get very excited as you are writing

- Find you have endless energy

- Many synchronicities continue to happen

- Feel the happiest you have felt in your life

- Writing your book brings healing to your life

Once you accept the Universe as your employer magical things happen everyday. Life becomes an adventure. You

NATURE ≠ EXERCISE 3

1. Write about one of your most magical experiences in nature.

2. What happened?

3. Reflect back to what was going on with you just before nature came into the picture.

4. Was your heart open? Was love flowing through you?

5. Was your heart closed? Did nature help it open?

6. What happened to you after your interaction with nature?

7. Did you feel excited, inspired, opened up?

8. Connect the dots—love, exchange, Universal Energy Flow, nature, grace, and you.

9. If you felt any step was missing in the experience, claim it now.

10. Call the experience back using your memory. Open to love and exchange with nature; receive the Universal Energy Flow and allow the grace to flow to you.

11. Do something good with it.

leave behind the mundane drama of worry, and negativity. You become full of enthusiasm. When this is all flowing and functioning you become crystal clear about life. It is possible for you to experience yourself on the spiritual plane while in a human body! Are you ready to think about this and give it a try?

This approach is about being grounded, present, and conscious in your body in every moment. This is about your choices in life. What are you choosing to experience with every choice you are making? Are your decisions coming from a place of love or are they coming from a place of fear, anger, or sadness?

When you are in the Universal Energy Flow and love is the vibration of all your actions, then grace flows very rapidly to you. There is an abundance of Universal Energy pulsing through your physical vessel. Healing occurs on all levels; physically, emotionally, mentally, and spiritually. You feel great! Your faith, which I define as trust in the Universe, grows because you are being exchanged with in a way you can rely on.

No human is in control of your love, exchange, energy, or spirit. You are free! Free to live, express, celebrate, love, and exchange with all that there is in existence. Infinity. To quote Martin Luther King, Jr., "Yes, free, free at last!"

SELF≠LOVE AS A CIRCLE

EXERCISE 4

Meditate on this Diagram of Love & Exchange depicting the completed circle of self-love and Universal Energy Flow.

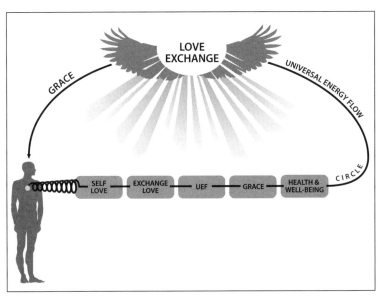

Diagram 8 – Self-Love as a Circle

In this example we start with you. As you love yourself energy generates through the heart and you fill yourself up with love. It spirals out of you and through conscious choice you start to exchange love with the Universal Energy Flow. This creates grace, which in turn creates health and well-being. When the life force is strong it allows an even greater connection to Universal Energy Flow. This circle creates an abundance of love and exchange from the Universe flowing back to you as grace.

I repeat, if you can get this idea of exchange into your reality then you will succeed at anything you choose to do. As your spiritual appetite increases, you have more love to give to yourself; this creates more exchange, and gives you even more energy, respect, appreciation, value, and money. Your level of enthusiasm demonstrated through your love, exchange and grace will be contagious. Others will gather round you to ask for your help and guidance. If you want to continue to operate at a high level of effectiveness in relation to Universal Energy Flow keep exchange balanced and conscious, then sit back and enjoy the ride. If you are not there yet, let me help you check in and explore some of the areas where you may be blocked.

This is where the work comes in.

DISCIPLINE

It takes discipline to develop on the spiritual path. Too few people impress me with their ability to be disciplined. Looking at human tendencies and being straightforward and honest about our basic limitations is not easy. The spiritual spiral of going deeper into yourself can be slow, and confronting.

When it gets gritty most people check out, or move on to something new. "New is better, it's more fun, it holds more potential than the old, it's the best!"

You are conditioned to be a consumer rather than doing the gritty work of getting to know you. Most are looking for the easy way. Try being a plumber for a day; no matter how hard you try not to, you're going to get dirty. Once you realize it is just part of the work, and it will all wash off, you can get on with fixing the pipes. Spiritual work takes discipline; sometimes it can feel like you are digging in the muck. Do the work; you will grow love for yourself in the process.

Like most experiences there is a honeymoon phase where everything is magical for a few months, and seemingly huge gains can show up during this time. I say seemingly because an experience may be based on many external stimuli that in the longer run an individual cannot replicate (i.e. having a certain experience/deep release in conjunction with a healer, therapist, or group of people and this fizzling out when alone, or not being able to get there). Learn to distinguish between getting high on someone else's energy, getting high on a group's energy, and exchanging with the Universe and filling your tanks with self-love. I cannot emphasize the importance of discipline enough.

> *Later in the book I will talk about one of my less desirable traits, which is rushing in life. I have learned that I have to slow down and let situations evolve, therefore spiritual discipline in my life has been something I have had to work at. I like the fireworks and the big experiences that the breath work can open up, but sometimes it is about the exercise of breathing, letting go of the mind, and simply relaxing. There*

may not be any fireworks this day, or for several days. The analogy I use about discipline is going to the gym on the days I do not want to go. Each and every bit of exercise hurts, and I might not stay long but after I feel better. All of this prepares me for the days I'm with the trainer, or need to perform athletically. The same with spiritual discipline; the days when I want to practice the least are the days where the biggest gains occur, because I am building discipline and respect for myself.

DISCIPLINE ⸱ EXERCISE 5

A six-month prescription for you:

1. Read this book and do all of the exercises—take your time with it!

2. Read *The Reluctant Healer* and do all of the exercises. People have reported miraculous healings just doing the exercises!

3. Learn the pranayama breathing meditation and practice daily, a minimum of seven-minutes per day. This will complement any spiritual practice you are already doing. You can download a free meditation MP3 on the Home Page of my website www.thereluctanthealer.com.

4. If you miss a day, jump back in the next. You will love this simple seven-minute practice and will feel lighter and more joyful immediately.

5. Let me know how your progress goes.

6. Discipline is key!

HUMAN NATURE

I wish I could start off with a statement about human nature that was more positive, but the truth is most humans are underdeveloped spiritually; underdeveloped because most have little consciousness or spiritual discipline in their life. A small percentage of humans are willing to connect the dots and see how X on a spiritual level affects things created on physical, emotional, and mental levels. This is what this work is about as we look at everything from the cause and effect of the spiritual plane. I see it as a science, albeit different from the science most are used to. If you know you have work to do with yourself in your own development as a spiritual being, or simply want to feel happier, then read on, I am sure you will gain something.

While existing in a human body, most of you can use healing on some level in your life whether it is physical, emotional, mental, or spiritual. Again if you are following here I may be preaching to the choir, and there is a good chance you have been on the spiritual path for some time. I acknowledge your appetite for growth and development. I ask you what I always ask everyone, "Are there any places where you feel stuck, or blocked in your life?" I have honestly never had anyone say, "There are no places." Most say, "Let me get my list!"

> Karrie, a 35 year-old, wine-merchant came to me because her boss bought her a session. She was reserved at first and said everything was good. I asked her, "Are there any places where you are stuck?" "How much time do you have?" she replied. The question always seems to hit home in people, and I ask it as early into the session as possible to avoid wasting too much

time on small talk. So we got onto addressing that list, and Karrie is moving forward.

It is important to know where you are in life in order to get anywhere. If you are stuck, it is important to first of all know you are stuck. Then it is important to know where you are stuck, and what would open up if you were not. It is important to know your blind spots, prejudices, and judgments because often they form the ceiling to your experience in this life. They are where you are stuck!

To be crystal clear, I believe our potential as human beings is unlimited. There is nothing we cannot achieve working to heal ourselves, working to heal others, and working together to heal our planet. Still I am under-impressed by the output I see most people living by. I say this in an encouraging way. I recognize our vast potential.

Larry, age 42, came to me depressed and unhappy. All he wanted to talk about was his past job as a news reporter. I asked him what happened and he danced around the question. I inquired again if being a news reporter was so important to him, why did he stop? He admitted that he was lazy and got fired from his last job. He was stuck beating himself up for messing up a good career. I told him to get over it; that he was still young and could do anything. He said he was interested in doing work as a reporter who inspired people and helped them in some way. As we discussed his desire more in depth, he found a true appetite to help people.

In our healing work together we focused on clearing his stuck emotions, mainly anger and sadness out of his gut. We accomplished this by working with his energy and I was amazed at how fast he became inspired and started contact-

ing people about work again. Within a short time Larry was back doing work he believed in, and his issues of self-loathing started to dissipate as he found himself more on purpose with his heart. It became clear to him that he had a spiritual purpose in life to do good, to help others, and to learn to love himself. He later told me he had found a job that turned him on so much he would literally jump out of bed in the morning to go to work. He said this was the job he had been waiting for his whole life, and he learned to love himself through the action of helping others.

If you want to feel content and truly happy, reach out your hand and help someone whether they are a cousin, neighbor, stranger, or enemy. As we help others heal we complete something inside of ourselves. Reaching for peace and harmony will always outweigh the benefits gained by fighting. At our highest pinnacle of achievement we will always be waging peace, not war. So, how do we move forward in these times of skepticism, unrest, and turmoil? How do we reach when there is so much fear? You consciously reach through the fear, reach through the skepticism, unrest, and turmoil. It may not be easy, but if you reach, healing will occur on individual, and group, as well as planetary levels.

Not everyone is interested in living a life full of conscious choice. If ease of life is what you are looking for, it is definitely easier in some ways to have less spiritual appetite and purpose. The more appetite you have for spiritual evolution, the more you will be forced to learn about yourself as a human being and, more importantly, as a spirit being. The more you will have to learn about detaching from human dramas and distractions. It is a tight wire act. The higher the wire the more confidence you will need in your balance and ability to stay focused in any situation.

Human existence is typically not viewed through the lens of the spirit, rather it is viewed through the lens of the physical experience of what is happening to you right now; or through the emotional lens of how familiar the emotion is—I like it, I am happy; I do not like it, I am not happy; or through the lens of the mind—I think therefore I am; my mind is my experience of all that is; there is nothing beyond my mind. Clearing karma and getting on with your spiritual life purpose is where true fulfillment lies, and this is where the biggest spiritual appetites are situated. It is not for everyone. Most people are not concerned with clearing karma because the distractions of being human are so occupying.

To truly heal, grow, evolve, and reach the point of contentment inside of ourselves through helping others, we also need to know ourselves as individuals, we need to know our human characteristics, and we need to know the potentials and limitations of the choices humans make. The more that is known, the more trust in assessing what our role in this process is. The deeper your relationship with yourself on the spiritual level, the easier it is to understand why you are here and what you are here to do.

A few basic limitations I focus on to help you know yourself better are the tendencies of being extreme, aggressive, driven by ego, addictive, and stubborn. As we delve into these areas I ask you to stay grounded; do the exercises and pay attention. If stuff comes up, e.g. you get frustrated, bored, or want to skip ahead, try not to. It means these areas need to be worked with. It is time to do this work, or you would not be at this page. Let's get started!

BEING EXTREME

Now that we are getting into the grittier aspects of being human, try to stay present to the information here. It will help you. Remember I am bringing this to you with a lot of love and precision!

Being extreme is related to the four other sections that follow, and they all come out of **not being able to fill yourself up with love**. I do not think I will get the point across if I just talk about love (positive). It feels necessary to speak about traits we exhibit when we do not feel love (negative), or when we look outside for love. Being extreme is a quality I have studied in people for many years and it comes out of a basic insecurity of not feeling love for self, and a desire to be loved by others at any cost. When the hole of insecurity leaks enough energy, people resort to extreme measures to feel 'safe,' 'in control,' 'perfect,' 'not bad,' or 'good enough' to be loved.

If you have an extreme nature you will consistently be marketed to in the ways I've listed below because you feel like someone else has the answers for you. When you experience vulnerability about how you feel about yourself, advertisers, people with something to sell, and negative energies have access to you. They can:

- ◆ Convince you something is wrong with you—you're not good enough to belong here! You require this or that to be happy.

- ◆ Tell you that you will become skinny and attractive doing a certain practice, eating a certain type of food, or following a particular diet

- Emphasize how sensitive you are and how much you are affected by other people's energy

- Promise you the secret to finding love, relationship, and money

- Spend lots of time talking to you about your enlightenment and tell you how gifted you are

When you come from a place of being connected to yourself, and trust in the Universal Energy Flow, then there will be no need to be extreme. There will be feelings of abundance, so it will be easy to exchange and play the game of life. If this is not the case, it is good to recognize it and do the work to find out why. When we define and understand behavior, it gives us the opportunity to grow.

As a teacher, I am careful not to influence people to work or study with me through their vulnerabilities. I do my best to try and not persuade them from any of these points. It is true that most people I work with are very sensitive, and I try to structure my work to give them room to choose without too much marketing or persuasion. My desire is to help them develop their own truth about their instinct, intuition and guidance. My work here is not about money, fame, or even recognition. My core motivation is to fulfill my spiritual life purpose to help people find their way and to receive the flow back from the Universe from a job well done. I do not want to hold onto people and, as I said in the first book, I am looking for leaders as opposed to followers. It is okay to not need me any more; as a matter of fact, I expect this.

Do you know the ways that you are extreme? Do you think this idea applies more to you, or to society as a whole?

If you are looking for love outside, do you set yourself up to be seduced, the seducer, the addict, the abuser or the abused? Think about it and do this next exercise.

EXTREME ⸰ EXERCISE 6

1. Write about the ways you feel like something is wrong with you.

2. Do advertisers have free access to your wallet by convincing you that your life could be a lot better if you bought their product?

3. What ways are you seducible because of being extreme?

Recently, I was at a car wash in Eagle Rock, California; it is always a good place to witness people in the real world. Many, including myself, use this time to return calls and find ways to look busy. Some read the newspaper, some eat ice cream, others peruse notices on the bulletin board, and all watch for their car to come out glistening. I notice people deciding how much of a tip to give the attendants for their skilled cleaning services.

As I am playing with my iPhone, this lady suddenly sits down next to me, and she is tense. She starts yelling at someone on her cell phone, and she is constantly checking her Lexus. This lady is intense! Finally the worker honks the horn and waves the red towel. She beelines her way to him waving her finger at him. She points at spots from the back bumper to the front of the car, and he is spit shining as he goes. She moves up to the windows and keeps insisting on some imaginary spots until he re-cleans all the windows inside and out. She has the poor guy running around frantically. People are starting to squirm in their seats; other workers are stopping to watch the show. Finally, she grabs her keys and hands him a folded up dollar bill.

I watch the whole thing because my car is sandwiched between her Lexus and another car. The worker unfolds the dollar bill as she drives off and just shakes his head.

I think of this scene numerous times, and I reflect on the extremeness in the energy and display of power by this lady. Are you ever like this woman in any way? As I think even more about this example, I admit that I have qualities that I consider to be extreme, not this extreme, but extreme enough for me to be aware of them.

One of these traits is rushing too much; therefore, I consciously work on slowing myself down, and having more patience. Sometimes this results in me driving too fast, so I have to pay attention when the Universe is telling me to ease up. Usually a bird will fly close to my windshield and when that happens I have learned to take my foot off the pedal immediately; there might be a cop around the next turn, and even more importantly, there may be a dangerous situation ahead. When I am rushing it can show up across the board, resulting in not enough patience and no time for gratitude and exchange with the Universe. Feeling as if I am short on time and rushing to catch up is ultimately draining because I miss the entirety of the moment.

The biggest healing I have learned about rushing is that it happens when I am not fully dealing with something in my life. Whatever situation I have ignored or swept under the rug is pulling on my awareness and energy. Once I stop and deal with the situation, time expands, and I no longer have the need to rush. When this happens I find I am not as seducible to being distracted, or becoming extreme. When I am present and slow down I feel like everything unfolds in divine timing and I feel content. Why rush?

I'll give an example to show you what I am talking about:

Several years ago I met Simon, age 62, who had a nice RV parked in front of the bank I use and it was for sale. The RV doors were open as a way of inviting people in to check it out. It was a pleasant, sunny Sunday afternoon and I thought I might as well take a look. I had been thinking about an RV for the first book tour. Simon was a good salesman and you could tell he was honest. He had all the bells and whistles on the RV plus he had taken excellent care if it. He knew it inside and out! We talked, I kicked the tires and I test drove it. We discussed money and I left to sleep on it.

A few days later, I stopped to see him at his house and met his wife. They told me about all of their trips. Simon asked me to put down a small deposit for him to hold the RV for me to see if I could get the rest of the money. It was Thanksgiving and I was headed to Kentucky for the holiday. The more I slept on it, the more I realized it was not that good of a deal, plus I was feeling like gas was going to be a problem soon. The more I thought about it the more tension I felt, and the Universe turned the heat up. Everywhere I looked, the signs the

Universe were sending appeared to contradict the purchase. I felt conflicted and my energy became quite extreme. I found myself rushing as I was driving and I was sharp with people because I was torn about dealing with Simon. I really liked him and some part of me felt bad about backing out of the deal, plus he had my $750 deposit.

Finally, when I was back from the holiday, I knew I had to make the call. He was disappointed and wanted to keep the deposit. We ultimately worked it out and things ended on good terms. Even though the RV could have been good for the book tour, it would have been a questionable investment. I was definitely lured into the experience because I was already thinking about an RV and Simon was a good salesman. My intuition pushed me several ways after I gave him the deposit and I realized the commitment was premature. Once I knew I had to deal with him, I hit against the possibility of a confrontation and this was the area I had to take responsibility for. I realized afterwards that stretching it out over the holidays had been a mistake because it kept me from being fully present with my family. I have since learned to deal with things that disturb my energy as soon as they come up.

I am far less extreme when I am dealing with my heart. When I am dealing with myself internally I am able to slow myself in each and every moment. Think about how much Universal Energy Flow it gives me when I notice the bird flying by my windshield, slowing my car down immediately, and not getting a ticket, or just missing an accident. Suddenly heaven is here on earth in these expanded moments where I am choosing my own reality; suddenly I am dreaming my reality into existence. All of my needs are satiated from the love of self. If this connection is not made my behavior goes sideways and becomes more extreme even to the point of aggression, which I will talk about in the next section.

If you 'rush around' in your life, how can you start to work with you? Can you slow down? Later in Section 2, I will be talking about intuition and how it plays a role in all of this. Remember the comment about the bird flying toward my windshield in the prior paragraph? Paying attention to this with my intuition has been some of the work I have done with myself. We will explore this later. Remember it is all connected.

AGGRESSIVE CONSUMERISM

There are other important limiting traits, characteristics, and behaviors that we have as humans. When behavior is extreme, we make unconscious choices and decisions; this fuels aggressive consumerism. Aggressive consumers have very little regard as to where the resources they consume are coming from. We want our needs met now! The truth is much of our consumption is wasteful and unnecessary. It does neither the earth, the environment, nor us any good. The 2008 statistics about the goods bought from retailers like Wal-Mart and the high percentage (up to 99%) of these goods that end up in the landfills within six months is astounding (www.storyofstuff.com). Meanwhile we are encouraged to 'keep shopping.' Let's face it. The machine is broken.

Yes, much of the world has been seduced into believing that the American way of thinking is more glamorous and is therefore more fun and fulfilling. But the illusion is becoming more and more precarious. As I write this the dollar is suffering and the U.S. economy is well...you know. The consumption is consuming itself and I am afraid that we are all in for a rude awakening.

Awakening? Am I truly speaking about an opportunity for you and me to wake up?

Think about just how different your experience is from your parents' and their parents' stories about their lives and more difficult times. Look how far we have come, and look how far we have fallen. No one wants to endure hardship. We do not want our children to suffer. Would you be willing to admit that you expect life to be easy? Does anyone in our country expect his or her child to suffer from a lack of nutrition, clean water, or simple medicine? I do not think so. Do we have gratitude for our food, water, and medicine? Not so much...we expect them. We expect life to be safe, predictable, and easy.

Life is changing rapidly. In my most humble opinion we have been partying at the expense of the Earth. I do not think it is business as usual. We have been living in a time of much illusion about resources, and the *exchange* with all inhabitants of the planet has been off.

Natural resources are finite and we are facing times ahead where this will be a bigger issue for all of us. For the sake of this discussion, I need to distinguish that natural resources are only one aspect of Universal Energy Flow, which I have described as infinite.

Rainbows will likely arc the sky long after man has vanished; stars will still blanket the heavens; the moon will light up the night; and the sun will shine, and the Earth will continue to spin on its axis. In other words the Earth is going to go on functioning without us. If a resource is gone, depleted, or abused, yes, we will have altered the Universal Flow in some small way, but the Universal energies will continue on just fine. For humanity, however, the consumption of resources and the pace in which the environment is changing is very rapid now. I am writing this to increase awareness of how we consume, of what we buy, and why we buy it so that we can deal with the root cause of what we are looking for: is it to feel good enough, worthy, valuable, loveable? Is it to fill up the hole that can only truly be filled with self-love?

Below is an old prophecy that I read quite often; a Cheyenne Indian called Sweet Medicine spoke it hundreds of years ago. Let it register, see what part of it could be speaking about your lineage, could be speaking about you:

After a long life of more than 100 years, Sweet Medicine called the tribe to him, for he was greatly troubled and knew that his time on Earth was drawing to a close. He told the gathered tribe that he had given them the instructions that they should live by, and that only if they continued to follow those instructions would they remain strong. But should they fall from those ways, all manner of trouble would beset them. This having been said, Sweet Medicine delivered his famous prophecy.

"There are many people on this Earth besides the Cheyenne and their Indian brothers. At the same time many people that you know nothing of shall come from the East. Some of them shall be black, but there will be a fair-skinned people, and they shall be numerous.

"These fair-skinned ones shall have hair much lighter than yours and they shall have hair upon their face. Their

customs and manners shall be very different from yours. They will come with their own ways of thinking, and they shall not pray to the Great-Grandfathers as you do. Listen to nothing they say. But I fear that, trusting them, you will listen.

"These fair-skinned ones are a restless people, and they are never satisfied. They do not know what it is to be content and grateful for all that the Great-Grandfathers and Grandmother Earth have provided. They will move quickly from one place to another, ever pushing forward, and more and more of them shall come. They shall not come to you only on foot, but also in strange things upon the rivers and in boxes upon the land. Their clothing shall not be like yours, but rather made of many pieces together and in many pretty colors.

"They shall offer you many things, like isinglass [a reflective object, such as the white man's mirror]. All that they offer you will do you no good and will begin to sap both the strength and the will of the People. Their food shall be strange, and they shall offer you something like sand to eat that shall be very sweet. Eat nothing that they give you, for none of it will be good for you. But worse of all, they will offer you a strange drink, and if you drink it you will go crazy. Unfortunately, you will like these things that the Earthmen bring, and more than likely you will take them. I warn you that if you do, your troubles will be never-ending. Take nothing from them. But I fear for you, and my heart is very heavy.

"These people will kill the animals and will uproot the Earth. The buffalo will be hunted down for sport. Our four-legged brothers and sisters will begin to disappear. They shall hunt them with a strange and powerful weapon – it shall be noisy, and from it will be sent something like a pebble, which will be deadly.

"When they come, they will bring with them their own kind of animal – not like the buffalo, but one with short, shiny hair, white horns, and split hooves. They will eat these animals, and so will you. There is another kind of animal that they shall bring, one with a long tail and hair about its neck. This animal will allow you to travel far. With the coming of this animal, your decline shall begin. That is what I fear.

"These people do not love Grandmother Earth as you do. They will dig her up and fly in her air. They may even take lightning from the sky so that where they live they can see at night. Ceaselessly they will search for a certain stone that our Great-Grandfather has placed on the Earth. They do not follow the ways of the Great-Grandfather, and they will dig and dig into the Earth to find this stone. They will kill our Grandmother Earth.

"I see unknown sicknesses coming to you. You will die off – maybe all of you will die. And worst of all, if any of you do survive, these people will want your flesh, the very children of the People. This you must never let happen, for, if you do, your children will become like them, and they will know nothing. These people are restless and will do all in their power to make you like them. They will not stop.

"My heart is saddened, for you will not remember what I have said to you – you will leave your religion for something new. You will lose the respect for your leaders and start quarreling with one another. You will lose track of your relations and marry women from your own family. You will take after Earthmen's ways and forget the good things by which you have lived, and in the end become worse than crazy.

"I am sorry to say these things, but I have seen them, and you will find that they come true."

By most accounts, Sweet Medicine died hundreds of years ago at Devil's Tower in Wyoming; by others he began his journey to the Spirit World just west of Bear Butte. No matter where, he ranks as one of the world's great spiritual teachers and prophets.
—*American Indian Cultural Heroes and Teaching Tales. Evenings With Chasing Deer by Kurt Kaltreider, Ph.D*

This prophecy speaks volumes to me because I feel the truth of who we are as a people today in it. We are restless, mostly unsatisfied, and generally ungrateful for all that we have available to us. It makes me sad to feel into the emptiness of most of the people I know. I tire of trying to help people connect to spirit, to the Mother Earth, to all the blessings we have. Endlessly I see some of the most aggressive behavior on the planet being displayed in pursuit of spiritual awakening. It seems that people feel justified to be as aggressive as they want to seek out the experience of spiritual awakening, healing, and enlightenment. It is amazing what people set out to desire, take, covet, own, and dominate in the name of God, or democracy for that matter.

I am only going to say this one time, so pay attention. I do not care what religion you practice, or what spiritual practice you ascribe to, because I work with all of them and see the commonality. If you are in a teaching that discriminates, or believes they are superior to others—be careful with that system. Remember it is human nature to be extreme and be marketed to in a way that causes separation and segregation in the world. Be wary of organizations if they try to control you through fear. Time here is too precious for this. Ultimately you will have to develop your faith in a way that works for you. I can promise you that developing yourself spiritually to connect to the Universe will help you heal, and will set you free.

> *Alex, a 24 year-old young man told me he was worried about his aggressive behavior. He had recently been to a spiritual event with his new girlfriend, Natalia. He liked her a lot and really wanted her approval. He got in a fight at the event over trying to secure some seats up close to the teacher. He had his reasons for doing what he did. He said he was doing it for Natalia, so that she could experience the teacher first hand. Ultimately they were asked to leave because other people were uncomfortable with his aggression. I explained to him that sometimes when we want to look our best is when we become most aggressive because of the investment to look good, or have something. I also told him I have witnessed people being very extreme and aggressive at spiritual events, and they are no different from concerts, or ballgames. It doesn't matter where we are, human behavior is the same when we want something. He said he apologized to Natalia profusely, but she has been too embarrassed to forgive him. I encouraged him to make amends, but first he needed to start with himself. If he could get the lesson now, he had a long road ahead to 'do good' in the world.*

Aggressive consumerism and aggression come from the same place. People are aggressive and act more aggressively when there is an empty feeling inside. No amount of external consumption is going to satiate that appetite, and the more your spirit pushes you to heal this condition, the more energy you will feel around it. The more revolution you feel inside, the more aggression!

Aggressive consumer
EXERCISE 7

1. Write down the areas where you know you have aggressive consumer energy (e.g. driving; being first in line anywhere; getting a parking spot at Wal-Mart; when you are hungry; when you are frustrated with electronics; over food and water when there is an emergency; around people who are less intelligent than you think you are, etc.). Make your list.

2. Write about the ways you feel justified to be the way you are because most everyone else is the same way.

We do not have to meet aggression with more aggression. I write this because I have felt the aggression, and it disturbs me. It disturbs me because I know I have it in me and I know it drives me to unconscious consumption. It drives me to rush. It drives me to judge and project onto those who act more aggressively than I do. When will we be able to address this disease as a culture? Does it happen one by one until a collection of consciousness rises up out of the ashes like the Phoenix?

I seek out peaceful ways to learn to co-exist. What is my role, what is yours? If you are reading this you probably have a role as a teacher, as a peace marcher, as a messenger, as a healer, as a writer, and as a student. We're all the same. Embrace them for they know *now* what they do!

I think about electronics and the aggressive consumerism displayed in the lines to get the first iPhone. Did you get rid of a perfectly good cell phone to upgrade to the iPhone, or the latest Blackberry? How important a role are electronics playing in our lives these days? Could we function without them? Do you get aggressive to have the latest gadget? Did you get the latest gadget because it was the cool thing to do?

What is the truth about technology? Is it stunting our connection to things in the natural world? Do they become addictive? How much do you gain from their convenience and necessity? How do you use them and not lose something?

I am an admitted electronic user. I do not know what I would do without my computer, iPhone, and iPod. I have consumed therefore I am! I try to keep things in perspective, although I wonder what role electronics will play in my daughter's life. With television and computers acting as the free babysitters, I am seeing so many young people isolate in the electronic age.

I talk about this because I am a consumer, albeit when I really want something I can be an aggressive consumer. I am an Apple fan and user and they are great at marketing. They sure know how to lure me in!

I rely on email, and use social networking tools. Have I arrived, or have I departed? Do not get me wrong, I am not in despair about electronics, but what is the truth about their effect on us? I am clear electronics are changing us rapidly— some better, some worse. For the better they allow us to work from home, communicate with the world, and be entertained endlessly. For worse they distract and take up much of our consciousness, they give off harmful energy that is not good for our well-being, and they cause us to disconnect from the natural world. Within this overall picture I would like you to think about how they affect you.

AGGRESSIVE CONSUMER MEDITATION ⁓ EXERCISE 8

1. Do the free breathing meditation mentioned earlier (p. 48), and set an intention to 'heal the aggression inside.'

2. As you start to tingle and vibrate, gently ask your mind to relax, ask your heart to open, and ask your spirit to guide you.

3. Ask your spirit to show you that you are safe and abundant.

4. Let the little child inside your heart feel safe and feel your love. Relax and enjoy the peace!

5. Take your time and exchange with the Universal Energy Flow.

6. Come back when you are ready.

7. Write down anything you experienced and what your spirit brought to you about your healing.

Most of us share aggressive traits both individually and collectively. As you continue on, stay focused, and find any small areas these negative traits may show up in you. Can you become more awake? If you are in denial you may have issues of addiction. Read on and see if we can bring more of these issues to light.

ADDICTION

Addiction is a topic I have been looking at for some time. It is closely related to being extreme and aggressive consumerism, but worthy of further mention. I look at addiction in a broader sense than just drug or alcohol dependency. I look at addiction from the perspective of habitual repetition of excessive behavior that a person is unable, or unwilling to stop, despite its harmful consequences to self or others. The root pathway that addiction takes into a person's experience of life is from the following negative thought forms:

- I am not good enough
- I am not enough
- Something is wrong with me
- I need to fix myself before I can do this…
- When I fix myself I will be able to do that…
- I need to fix somebody else
- If I eat better I will be happy
- When I am skinny I will be happy
- If I buy new clothes I will look good and be happy
- If I look good someone will love me
- When someone finds me and I have a partner I will be happy

And on and on and meanwhile seduction—its co-pilot—
joins the act. As long as you think there is something wrong
with you, you will be easily seduced and on the lookout for
the quick easy fix from the belief that someone else knows
better. Any time you are being seduced, there is an addiction.
The addict looks willingly with a blind eye towards the truth
and chooses not to see. The addict plays into being seduced,
and then feels justified about being angry when what they
were expecting doesn't get delivered (e.g. love, happiness, being healthy, skinny, etc.).

The point I am making is, the pathway for addiction is
through the hole of negativity one feels within. This hole is
created by no self-love. It leaks your energy, sometimes all of
your energy. There is no container for spirit while this hole of
inadequate feelings is draining your life force.

It is not about other people and what they did to you, it is
about what you are doing to you by not loving you!

The leaking hole of negative feelings is a downward spiral
of energy that accelerates when you give up on yourself, a sinking feeling. This is where the victim refuses to take responsibility for their creations. Or more to the point, this is the place
where victims refuse to create a new experience for change.

Yes, I am calling a victim an addict. Much of the time a
victim is an addict who uses seduction to try and get what
they want (i.e. enough love from the outside to fill themselves
up). If love is not available any substitute will do. Often this
gets them attention. For someone with victim energy, attention is synonymous with love.

Is this true for you?

In other words a victim is very good at magnetizing energy albeit oftentimes negative energy, and in some twisted

way the victim will associate this energy as love because it garners attention. This is why a victim will stay in relationship with an abuser because it is easier to get familiar energy from familiar sources, even if these sources appear abusive. But who is abusing whom? The victim is a master at magnetizing disapproval (thus getting energy) from a partner, friend, or family member. Notice, I am mentioning close relationships. Why would this occur so close to home? Because the addict needs someone to blame, someone to take responsibility for their pain, someone to enable them – and who better than someone they love, or say they love, or say loves them?

This is a fairly hard line here! Have you ever tried working with addicts and addiction? It is a very tricky energy to confront and deal with. If you have worked with these people, or if you have addiction problems, you'll know freeing yourself from this will take firmness and focus.

All of these limiting negative human qualities stem from the same place, no self-love.

Betsy, a 45 year-old housewife came to me complaining about Fred, her husband of 15 years. Betsy said she had to nag him to get anything done around the house, he had a terrible temper, and he might be having an affair. I asked her why she was with him? She said he loved her. I asked her how do you know? She said when he is not angry, and does things around the house he shows his love. I said what about the affair? She said that might be the real sign she should be looking at.

Betsy said she did not want to leave Fred, he was a good provider, and at least she had someone. Again I said what about the affair? She said someday she would deal with it, and hoped that it would go away. I talked with Betsy about loving herself, and I explained she put a lot of emphasis on Fred. She said that's what relationships are for, and that they are work. I agreed and kept encouraging her to do the work to develop herself. She said, "I just want to feel better today. I do not necessarily want to change. If I change I might have to leave Fred. I can't do that." I asked, "Why not?" She explained that he needed her. I said, "It sounds like he needs someone else, too."

Betsy refused to look at her potential to love herself and be happy. I stopped nudging her. This was the reality she was determined to hold onto. We worked from there.

Interestingly enough Betsy came back to see me two years later. Fred had left her for the other woman. Betsy got her wake up call, but even then she was desperate to hold on to the idea of Fred coming back. I told her, "You have to let him go. Your addiction to Fred, your dependency on him helped drive him away. You need to deal with you." She asked, "How?" I told her, "We have to start with you and build from the place of you loving you." She said she was not ready to do that work and she did not want to let go of Fred. I told Betsy that I am a patient man, and I could not make her issues mine. I let her know that when she was ready to do the work I might be around. If not, at least I would leave a book for her! I have not heard back.

Danielle, age 51 and an admitted addict enabler, routinely sees me one to two times a year to review her most recent rescue project. They are always the same – gorgeous, attractive hunks, who are addicted to heroin, meth, or crack. Each time she gets lured into the charm, charisma, story, and potential of *this special person. Each time I have to remind her of the last person who ended up stealing her car, TV, or heart. She tries to convince me that this one is different. I laugh and tease her about writing a romance novel. Of course she knows one day she will have to deal with herself, but in the mean time she keeps her life interesting with her next distraction.*

ADDICTION ⋆ EXERCISE 9

Remember addiction is a habitual repetition of excessive behavior that a person is unwilling, or unable to stop, despite its harmful consequences to self or others.

1. Write down the areas where there is addiction in your life (Alcohol, sex, sugar, nicotine, caffeine, drugs, TV, money, Internet, clothes, caretaking, control, stress, relationship, love, etc.).

2. In each area try to answer what you are seeking. What are your deepest thoughts around these addictions? Do your best to get to the bottom of each one.

3. What did you find out? Does it all come down to feeling like you are not going to be loved? That love will leave you? Are you angry about not being loved?

All of these limiting, negative traits stem from the same place, no love of self. You have to learn to love yourself. You have to learn how to patch and heal the internal hole so that you can keep your reservoir full with love and self respect.

I realize this is some hard-hitting material, but remember dealing with addiction takes firmness and focus. Do you have addictions? I have worked with lots of addicts; they all share these same issues. It seems they can only hear the truth when they want to hear it, or when they hit rock bottom. I do my best to hold firm with them and tell it like it is. You win some and you lose a lot more until a person is ready to do the work.

Now, let's look at how the ego can be destructive in certain relationships.

EGO

The ego can be defined as the personality or self-image, oftentimes associated with an inflated opinion of oneself. It has an incredibly powerful way of controlling your emotions, and if you are driven by your emotions you will rarely know when the ego is distorting your point of view. The elixir of the emotional energy and the justification for the emotion gives the ego the space to control you. Typically this dynamic becomes most powerful when you have created a karmic relationship of great depth, meaning you have a person in front of you who is helping as a teacher, relationship partner, parent, boss, etc.

Take note if this is a person you have experienced great passion and love for, the ego will set you up to kill this person off! The ego wants you for itself. If indeed you have felt safe with this person for one second, if your heart started to open, your ego will start to funnel your karma into the relationship, projecting deeply buried emotions that have not seen the light of day for some time. If you are on a spiritual path, and you have done some work on healing your emotions, what a great time for the ego to step in and convince you to flex your newfound freedom onto this relationship. 'This person is safe for me. I have the right to express these things to them. They encourage me to express myself. They are the one doing this to me! I feel empowered expressing my anger to them! I am really growing now!'

This is the trap with the ego, it tricks you into thinking you have free reign to express your emotions in a destructive way. This is how the ego likes to play! Instead it oftentimes means that you have to be even more conscious of your emotions in all your relationships. This is one of the challenges along the road of enlightenment; the more conscious you become the steeper the path you may travel, and likely the more people who will want to use you as a mirror.

Jeff, a 45 year-old social worker came to me complaining about his sister, Jessica. He was very upset. They had always been close, but were estranged now. Jessica was going through a divorce and things had become difficult. Jeff said Jessica was really going through it and the whole family was tired of hearing about it because Jessica was expressing so much hostility and anger towards everyone. And to make it worse Jessica was a therapist and Jeff thought she should be handling things better. With her being a therapist, and him being a social worker, you would think it would have helped. But the situation was a disaster!

Jeff said Jessica used all of the terminology to spit out her venom. He said she cut him to the bone, so he cut Jessica out of his life because of her abuse. He said he felt guilty because he knew she was struggling and he could not help her. Eventu-

ally most of the family limited their time with Jessica. It took about a year for Jeff and Jessica to reconnect. She was mad at everyone during this time, because she was forced to go deeper into relationship with herself, and she felt alone. Eventually she admitted that her ego had just about destroyed all of her relationships during this time. She confided that she had also grown addicted to a lifestyle her husband had promised her, and had hungered to be rich. When her husband failed in business her hopes were dashed. She became desperate and angry. Fortunately time does heal many rifts between family members. Eventually Jeff reported that he and Jessica healed their relationship because they had the skills to communicate in a healthy and respectful way. As long as they did that everything worked out.

Oftentimes the ego is going to cause a spike in the emotions and this behavior is tied to the release of the energy of something that has been suppressed in the body and consciousness for a long time. That is why it can appear so distorted when it finally surfaces. This can be exemplified as destructive anger, the manic energy associated with depression, or the panic energy with anxiety. Often it is a force that blows situations out of proportion, sometimes marking the end of relationships prematurely, which again is a result of the ego.

Tom, a 43 year-old MD, came to me complaining about his wife, Lori. He said she has lots of problems, but that she had always maintained peace towards him during their time together. Recently she had become more and more hostile and abusive. It was like she was trying to drive him away. He said he still loved her and wanted to work it out.

I listened to Tom's story and felt like there were many things going on, the biggest being that he was becoming more and more successful. Lori was insecure that she was going to lose him and she was working at pushing him away. Tom agreed.

Lori was open to couples work, and I found her to be in better shape than Tom described. We uncovered the areas they were stuck in the relationship. Tom gave Lori some reassurance that he was not going anywhere, and she settled down, let more help in, and became peaceful towards Tom. Eventually they united on the spiritual path, and committed to doing their spiritual practices and healing together at least once a week. Over time I have watched Lori heal deep-seated issues within herself and Tom has grown more successful, and their relationship has blossomed because they did not allow the ego and emotions to create any more problems between them.

The most important partnerships in your life may be more encompassing than sexually romantic relationships. The truth is, in some of your most important relationships you may not be romantic partners at all. The passion you feel is from your essence in recognition of what you share for each other as teachers, friends and partners on a mission to help set other souls free. You may have purpose beyond the physical, emotional, and mental—you may have a spiritual purpose together to be able to demonstrate peace and love within your community. That may be your role in helping others heal.

In Tom and Lori's case there was enough passion and agreement to remain together as romantic partners. That is how the picture looked from the outside. I know they worked it out and stayed together because they came together on the inside. They secured spiritual love deep within themselves when they started their practice together, and it opened all the vistas for them to remain happily together in a beautiful way.

Lori had been pushing the relationship in all the obvious ways that ultimately led them to healing. She was a catalyst. I can attest that in many, if not the majority of relationships, this is a role women step into. In a broader, more encompassing way, we can say that the feminine energy will be the catalyst to create spiritual movement in relationships more times than not. It is a compliment!

If your partnership involves raising children, your role at home may be to guide your children to honor the deeply polarizing karmic relationships known as family. Wouldn't it be amazing to teach your children how to free themselves? How to honor the teachers that they attract into their lives to evolve their essences into complete expressions of love? To get to these heightened levels of reality, you have to be able to get beyond the limiting influence of the ego.

A well-known healer I knew many years ago confided in me about his biggest problem in life. He said he always attracted gifted people who wanted to dedicate their life to him and his work. He said these people would show up as regular as clockwork, one or two per month. They would have the exact skill set he needed for his next project. All of the people had similar characteristics, they were on the spiritual path, and they had been looking for the right teacher for a long time. More often than not, they were better-than-average-looking women. They had decided on him, coming with the intention of service, commitment, and desire to learn.

This healer realized he had a vulnerable spot for women with a vagabond's free spirit. He would take them in, give them food and shelter, and hope they would deliver on the agreed upon exchange. For years the promise was always to help him get his material organized so that he could write his book. His question to me was, "Why don't they ever live up to their end of the bargain?" I saw they would immediately have a love/hate relationship with him. He would quickly become the father figure to women and men alike, and when he got lazy he would have sex with the women. The final result would be some misunderstanding and the relationship would end.

I told him to stop having sex with his students, and to try and actually finish his book himself. I got to know several of the people who worked with him, and found out that he had indeed helped to get all of them unstuck in their life. Every single one! Their lives opened up, they got what they wanted from him and moved on. He had lessons to learn about boundaries, and sexual energy. Nevertheless he had a powerful ability to help people get unstuck. His ego would always set him up to receive the short end of the stick with these people, and many of those who entered his life left angry and hurt. Yet for some reason, the experience with him would be the catalyst for them to open up and heal core issues.

Fortunately, he received the lesson, too. He realized he had to do the work and get his material organized. As he accomplished this, his work cleaned up and his book became a very well read self-help book known to many. He had to confront his own resistance to do the work around his creativity and expression; he became much more disciplined in his life.

Doing this work cleared up the areas that had been giving him trouble.

EGO ⸰ EXERCISE 10

1. Write about one relationship in your life when you felt the greatest addiction in all of your behaviors.

2. What were you looking for in this relationship? What was your ego looking for?

3. What kept you in it?

4. Are you still looking for what you thought you were going to get?

5. Was your addictive behavior due to you, the other person, or both?

In relationships where the ego and emotions tend to run the show and create negative behavior there is one remaining characteristic that comes into play. It can be challenging to move out of old patterns and into the new. Many have played this game. It is called being stubborn.

BEING STUBBORN

Stubbornness is definitely a common human characteristic! I have seen so many people who refuse to let go of someone, something, or some situation no matter how crazy it is. No matter how much abuse is being inflicted the question is why do people hold on stubbornly? Why do they love to suffer, and tell their story? How interesting do they think their story really is to those who have heard it a million times? Those around someone caught in this cycle usually start to feel abused and resentful over time. They get tired of being the energetic lunch box, and they develop survival mechanisms such as using caller ID to avoid certain people, 'emergency' situations on standby to get away, teammates ready to run interference, etc.

I am continually amazed at how long self-destructive behavior can persist in someone. There are many factors that come into play in these scenarios, some of them are:

- People associate love and pain synonymously

- People love to share stories about their pain

- People gather energy from others when they are in pain

- These same people hate being called 'victims'

- They are stuck in the adrenaline rush of war

- They will stubbornly hold on, take down the ship and feel justified about their righteousness

- They will hold on to the point of creating disease

- Some will hold on to the point of death

- Are you one of them?

If you are thinking about someone else in this moment that exhibits any of these traits, take this opportunity to thank them for being a mirror into your own stubbornness. Set them free.

A reporter once asked me, "Why don't people heal?" I explained to her people get addicted to the attention about their story of pain and abuse. The stress and worry become comforting. People can be very complex because they are unaware of their subconscious when they are being stubborn. We want to be fed energy when we want it, and we want it the way we want it, and we want to be able to let this serve as a pale substitute for love. People caught in this cycle of confusion have no reality about what love truly is.

If you are not one of these people do not worry, I am not talking to you. However, most of us can relate.

Just think about the chaos in the world, in this country, on the news, in your city, in your neighborhood, on your street, in your house, or even inside of you. Why the chaos? Why the drama? This way of getting attention is not love, and it never was! Why stubbornly hang on to the idea that there was the potential for love there?

"But you said you loved me!"

Stubborn people are tyrants about trying to get their self-imposed needs met. They will spend all of their collected energy trying to convince you and everyone else about their position. It never works because it is built through the manipulation of the ego, concocted by the mind and supported by the emotions. The position of reasoning is very rigid. It needs a shaky foothold of logic to support it, and frankly it is a position that lacks spirit, love, and light.

So, if you find yourself stuck, stubbornly hanging on to a position, or constantly needing to be right with someone—even yourself—give it up! Let go of control, let go of the outcome, let go of the past, let go of the feeling, let go of the future, just let go! Something interesting and fun is right around the corner for you if you can relax and have faith about your value to the Universe. Self-love is again the key to letting go and having faith, whereas no self-love will create endless stubbornness.

BEING STUBBORN ⚹ EXERCISE 11

1. Just check in with two people—Mom and Dad.

2. Write down anything you have to forgive, forget, let go of, and heal with them. Then do it.

3. If you cannot do this, then you are holding them accountable for something you need to deal with inside of you. More than likely there is stubbornness in this position. Let it go. When you set them free with love it will open up the next layer of intimate relationships around you, or waiting to come around you. It is time.

Linda, a 31 year-old artist was stubborn and stuck. I told her she enjoyed being angry. She was continually creating father figures to be angry at and of course, when I pointed this out, she got mad at me for a while. Then one day she returned and said she did not want to be stuck any more. She realized she was angry with her father, but did not know how to set him free. I suggested she make a list of the ways she was just like her father; she got mad at me again and said I am not like him in the least! I asked her if he was stubborn. She said of course! I said number one; continue writing down the ways you are just like him. She said it would take a while and she did come back to see me a couple of months later. Her list was quite long. Eventually she found the way to open her heart to herself through opening it towards her father. She became much more open and approachable. Her career took off, and her art began to sell. Love entered her life because it had a place to go inside of her. Her art became breathtakingly beautiful at this point, and to her new boyfriend, so did she.

Lee, a 39 year-old attorney recently asked me why it was so hard for him to change. Since I had known him for a while I thought he was ready to hear more about himself, or he would not have asked me this. I explained to him that he was very stubborn, and he liked to be in control. He gave me a cool smile and remained silent. I told him he was aggressive about getting his way and was fearful about the unknown. I softened it by saying that this was human nature, however I sprinkled in a little salt by telling him he was more extreme than the norm. He asked how to be more open to change. I suggested that he let go of control, embrace the unknown, and step forward with faith into the space of not knowing. He was skeptical. I told him to trust the Universe. He said that was easier said than done, and that he did not know if he had any faith, and did not know if he ever would. I told him he might never change then.

In his best lawyer approach he asked me to help him create a step-by-step practice that would guarantee him change. I told him it was up to him, not me. Used to getting his way, Lee said, "I admit to the things you have said about me, but isn't there a quick fix? Can we do the 'breathing thing'? Maybe I am ready for change." I smiled inside and released him to the breath. He was put on a schedule to breathe every day for 30 days. He extended his commitment several times, and reported slow change over several months. At least he had discipline! I saw more change with Lee than he reported and I kept encouraging him. He stayed with the breathing and that was my main direction to him over the last few years. I trusted the Universe to work with Lee to implement the right change and he is very happy with his life now!

REVISITING EXCHANGE

Exchange – The flow of consciousness given and received as energy, respect, value, appreciation, and love. It can also refer to goods, services and money.

Let us take another look at exchange. In all negative situations and circumstances exchange is off, and not balanced.

REVISITING EXCHANGE
EXERCISE 12

If you have felt any place inside of you where you are:

- Extreme

- Aggressive

- Addicted

- Driven by ego

- Stubborn

go back and review exchange.

Once you find balance in the way you exchange with others you will heal. As you heal you will become more conscious. Your life will become clear, people will be forgiven, transgressions will be forgotten and set free. Love will flourish in ways you have been longing for.

Do it, do it now.

Let the work begin, and please realize that, in most instances, I am talking about fine-tuning the work you have been doing, or trying to do your whole life. I give you credit!

Ellen, 50, a single mom had a relationship with a male friend, Tom, who loved her for years. She considered their relationship a friendship, he dreamed for more. There were always expectations and sticky situations that would arise because Tom wanted to be around and would offer to do things, but he would feel taken advantage of by Ellen when more was not delivered. This went on for years. She would dangle the carrot without the payoff of intimacy and sex Tom had waited for.

Finally I told Ellen the exchange was off. If she never intended on loving him romantically, she should clear the air with Tom. Maybe it would be better to pay him for his time when he helped out. They eventually worked out a financial exchange for the help he provided and this allowed their friendship to be honored. Ellen finally told Tom she never intended on sleeping with him, that she loved him as a friend. Tom finally let go of his dream; he dropped out for a while, but has since returned as a friend, and the space around them is much cleaner today.

MORE LOVE

We all need love to live; we all need love to evolve.

Love is the fuel that connects us to our essence. It sets us apart as one of the higher life forms of sentient beings on the planet. For better or worse, we are the center of our own Universe; however, when we are connected to love we expand beyond the human expectation. There is something really unique about the Power of Love. The Power of Love is the true miracle maker. Love transcends the physical linear levels, because love is not measurable, controllable, or predictable by logic or science. Love is the doorway along the spiritual path to the Divine.

Any complexities around love are created by the mental and emotional insecurities of humans. People can make love complicated, but love is not complicated. Love is light, and love is pure. In its purest form love lifts you up through the physical, through the emotional, through the mental to the spiritual. Once connected to the spirit it can lift you into direct alignment to the perfectly balanced energy of the Divine, the Universal Consciousness of all that is, and the creative principle that is still birthing the Universe in which we exist.

Logic, science, and the need to understand often live in an insecure, fear-based place. We do not trust the Power of Love. We want to own it and control it, which is actually the Love of Power. We want to dominate it for our own benefit. We want to feel good when we want to feel good. We want to feel loved by others all the time. Fear keeps us from fully releasing into love, and this is why 'love' is so frustrating for those who do not trust it.

MORE LOVE ~ EXERCISE 13

1. Write about your concept or understanding about love. What does it feel like? Can you trust it?

2. How much of it is defined by what your parents showed you?

3. Do you know you need to expand your trust about what love really is?

4. Does the idea of loving yourself still confuse, frustrate, or elude you?

The true quandary at play here is most of us do not know what love is. We know what we have determined love to be from our family, romance novels, movies, friends, and life experience. It is like the old saying: 'The goldfish knows about the ocean from its little glass tank.'

Let me say this again, love is the frequency that connects us to the Universe. Love is the true miracle maker when you allow it to flow into you from the Divine.

True love is Universal; it is not based on another human being. The love that flows through us to each other is not you and me, it is the allowance, the choice to let go and let the Universe flow through us. I repeat it is not you, it is not me, but rather the choice to allow something bigger than either of us to flow through each of us to the other. What we can control is the choice to let it flow, the choice to recognize the Universal Energy Flow in each other, and the beauty is in the recognition of the expression. How we choose to sparkle and vibrate with that energy, which is available to all, equally, is our choice.

No one is truly special to the availability of love. It is equal to all of us. No one determines how we are in relationship with love. We are the masters of our own choice to be love. No one else! When you get that, you can be free of negativity. Love is! Love is accessible equally to all of us, and through us into everything we do, especially our artistic expression. That is why I am choosing to direct so much healing through the creative realm, which is running on the cleanest human, green, sustainable, eco-friendly fuel—LOVE.

SHARING LOVE ≈ EXERCISE 14

1. Write down the ways you love yourself more since starting this book.

2. Share this with someone.

Ricki, age 42, has changed so much in the twenty years I have known her. In the beginning she was a young girl who was searching for her identity. In the last ten years I have witnessed her get married, settle down and give birth to two children. Love, relationship, and motherhood have taken her happily into middle-life. She has often said her husband has healed her, her babies have healed her, and maturity has healed her. I have happily agreed, and added that she has healed herself.

I remind her that she has savored the changes in life that many resist. She has loved her stretch marks, loved changing diapers, loved cooking, loved cleaning, loved being an artist, loved her husband, loved getting older – which is to say, she has just loved! We joke that she's too busy to fight. Most importantly, Ricki knows she's a lover.

The Power of Love is like a hummingbird; it cannot be captured or controlled. It has to be allowed to be free. If you allow the Power of Love to lift you up and bring sparkle and luminescence to your life—look out!

SUMMARY

To summarize my point of view here early on in this book, there are many ways to experience life. For many it may be even easier to live in a negative experience of life, instead of a positive one. The key to **healing** and the key to everything—health, well-being, life, spirit, connection, faith, and enlightenment—is about you being able to love. If you do not like you, you cannot love you. This is ground zero, the starting point for your work.

If you are playing small by living in fear, you never have to be accountable. If you choose to be an underachiever people will expect a lot less from you. If you are going to be totally accountable for all of your creations and experiences in life you will need to have great awareness with exchange. The positive aspects of life that exchange allows include: love, connection to Universal Energy Flow, grace, health and well-being, creativity, balance, expression, and clarity about your purpose. The more negative aspects of life, which are more common and widespread, include lack of self-love, extremeness, aggressive consumerism, addiction, ego and stubbornness.

I realize I am stating a lot of negative-sounding characteristics, but be honest…which of these define your experience of life? Is it time to change? Time to evolve, open up, grow, and release the past? You and I both know that it is.

> *The less you associate with some people, the more your life will improve. Any time you tolerate mediocrity in others, it increases your mediocrity. An important attribute in successful people is their impatience with negative thinking and negative acting people. As you grow, your associates will change. Some of your friends will not want you to go on. They will want you to stay where they are. Friends that do not help you climb will want you to crawl. Your friends will stretch your vision or choke your dream. Those that do not increase you will eventually decrease you. —Colin Powell*

Nothing in your life is going to bear fruit until you learn to love yourself and make contact with your heart and the love that flows through it. You have to learn to feel love for yourself. You have to be able to feel the smiles for yourself in your heart. Self-love connects you to everyone and everything. Once you love yourself you can effectively move out into the world and love others. Love makes you Universal. It is the foundation by which to understand life. It connects you to the Masters who walked the earth. "Love thy neighbor as thyself" will begin to make sense when you have learned to love yourself; it cannot happen if you do not. For love to exist in your world it has to happen inside of you first, then it can propagate 360 degrees around you. You become a circle, a Universe of love. Can I be any more emphatic, or clear about this!

Now…how to do it, right?

It is a feeling combined with the choice to love, and it is not something you pull back based on who you are around, how much you weigh or whether you're having a good day or a bad one. Self-love is constant. The ability to sustain this expression of consciousness results in an experience of true personal illumination. The prescription I follow is:

1. *I know I am a good person in my heart.* No matter what happens in my life I have this feeling secure inside of me. This good feeling enables me to make choices that consistently express the love I feel inside, and this keeps me exchanging with the Universe at all times. There is a flow of movement and energy happening because of this exchange. At times in my younger years when I was angry with my father, no matter how much I was rebelling, I still knew I was a good person. Love still flowed through me. Love is stronger than anger.

2. *I do not give my ability to love away to another person.* I keep my ability to love inside of me. My choice to love is between the Universe and me, not you. I set you free. I love you no matter what. My choice to love you does not depend on you loving me back; it depends on me just choosing to love.

   When someone pulls on my personal energy and I know I have to set a firm boundary, no matter how strongly I need to make this boundary, I keep love as the primary feeling generating inside of me. Even when the adrenaline is pumping I choose to let go of any fear and anger, and instead choose compassion to express my boundary.

Ultimately enough compassion will change to love, and love is my choice, my prescription.

3.   *One of the primary ways I connect to the Universe and my own inner love is through nature.* When I am choosing love in the face of adverse conditions, nature dances in front of me, it distracts me and focuses me into the spiritual realm at all times. Choosing love takes discipline and the payoffs are enormous because the Universe rewards me with the love from nature. Nature shows up for me in the city, in high rises and on concrete, just as much as it does when I am in the country. Love and nature set me free.

4.   *Play and fun nourish my loving spirit and unleash my feelings of love and joy.* I choose to have as much fun in my life as possible! I have so much fun exchanging love with my daughter, Ruby. She brings sparkle to my eyes when I think about the way she comes into the living room to scare me every morning. She always thinks she sneaks up on me, and I am very good at playing along. I love having fun when I am teaching, living, doing just about everything in my life, even writing. If I am not having fun I will not do something very long. If I did not love myself, I would not love to play so much. It is true that I like to tease, and I like to express my love playfully through teasing. I may be the only person who thinks I am funny, but at least I laugh at my jokes. The example I choose to live by is to not be too serious about anything.

5.   *Now create your prescription for self-love!* These are my primary moment-to-moment practices around love; through them I am fed a steady diet of positive optimism

from the Universe. As I always say, "The Universe has its own curriculum for me as well as you. I am always in the classroom." As long as I stay conscious of this I am in constant exchange with the Universe.

Loving myself allows me to express love freely, which taps me into the Universal Energy Flow, because love is the Universal language for us.

Andrew, 42, a self-professed loser came to me claiming he had one more try in him. I said, "The pressure's on, huh?" I'd said it referring to myself, however he took it as meaning him, and he started to cry.

He said his whole life everyone told him how creative he was, how unique, and artistic. Somewhere around age 25 he broke down, lost his confidence and gave up. His situation was extra-complex because he lived off a trust fund. He did not need to develop a relationship with money, he was conditioned to think he did not need exchange. All of his financial concerns were handled to the point of handicap. He was desperate because he had lost all passion for life.

Interestingly enough he had come into his inheritance in his early twenties, and was able to accept that the trust fund had affected his life in more ways than he was aware. I explained about exchange, and told him my sense was he had no exchange present; as a matter of fact he was in a resentful place, literally the opposite of exchange. He hated life, family, money, and responsibility. There were stipulations with the trust fund he had rebelled against from the beginning. So, the question boiled down to: are you willing to walk away from your dependence on the trust fund and trust the Universe to support you to become an artist again?

I did not ask him to join a cult, I did not tell him to leave his family, or kill them off in some way. I told him he needed to re-enter his life, to open his heart, create some faith through his willingness to give and receive through his creativity. To see where exchange could take him. What did he have to lose? Why not try it for a year? Surprisingly he agreed and deferred all of his interest income from the fund to charities and causes he believed in for twelve months.

His family thought he was crazy at first, but were relieved when they saw Andrew becoming alive again. He started playing music and became very active in playing and promoting his tunes. Things opened for him because he put his talent out there and it was exchanged with. His life turned around and he found the Universe would more than support his financial needs, which were not that excessive now that he was exchanging awareness around his consumption. He even reported his family had begun to trust him and offered him more flexibility with the resources. After three years he is still choosing to release these resources to charitable causes. However, he is no longer burdened by the control he once felt about family, money, or his trust fund.

REVIEW CHECKLIST

How are you doing with these exercises?

Self-Love Exercise:

- Be conscious of all the ways you love yourself.

- Work at this every day – review your list of the ways you love yourself and add to it as new ways appear.

Exchange Exercise:

- Write down the areas where you feel abundantly appreciated, and valued.

- Exchange in a positive way with the Universe, and this will give you self-love (Smile at the birds singing outside your window, tell the clouds how beautiful they are, blow kisses to the rainbow, hug a tree, sing to the stars, let the sun shine into your heart, etc.). As you actively exchange in the simplest ways with nature and the Universe you will feel self-love.

Discipline Exercise:

A six-month prescription for you.

- Read this book and do all of the exercises – take your time with them!

- Learn the pranayama breathing meditation and practice it daily, a minimum of seven minutes per day.

- Let me know how it goes!

If you work at these three simple exercises a few minutes every day, and let this become present in your consciousness, you will heal. Let's go!

section two

THE WORK

The Work

DEVELOPING YOURSELF AS YOUR OWN HEALER

My commitment to you is to help you find your way forward to yourself as your own healer, teacher, guide, psychic, mystic, friend, and partner. If I can accomplish this I will consider it a good day's work!

Two of the ways I have healed, and empowered myself have been through expressing and developing my intuitive gifts and creativity. This has resulted in increased confidence, trust, and faith in all areas of my life. If you can study this next section and do the homework, you will uplift yourself. Your faith can grow through the roof, and your ability to exchange love with the Universe will become a daily adventure. I promise you it will be the best investment of your life!

INTUITION – PART 1

According to the Encarta dictionary the general definition for intuition is: *the state of being aware of, or knowing some-*

thing without having to discover or perceive it. (When instinct reveals itself) without actual evidence. I agree with this definition, but I think it only scratches the surface.

Intuition is not about the head; it is not about figuring anything out. It is from a much truer source, the heart. If you know your heart based on the work you did in Section 1 and can trust yourself to open it to all the flows of energy around you, your intuition can flourish. However, how do you go about this if your brain governs you, if you are blocked physically, or have too much fear to let go of control? How do you access your heart?

For instance, in this moment my brain is trying to convince me to give up the desire to bring you the power and freedom associated with intuition. It is reminding me of the countless people I have worked with who will probably never give up their fear and addiction to the control of the ego working in conjunction with the brain. Letting go of that control takes faith and a willingness to trust that you are guided by higher powers in the Universe.

"But wait a second," asks your brain. "What does that mean?" It means that there are Universal forces present in every moment that are giving you guidance, signs, direction —intuition about everything! You are never alone. **The ego and brain want you to think that you are all alone.** The ego and brain drive the emotional response in your body when you are in a place of negative emotion—anger, fear, and sadness. When you are in a place where you are connected to the Universe your emotions flow in a pure form and you feel positive, loving, joyful, and serene. Go ahead and think about it! This is why it feels so good to be in love. When you are in love things flow easily, there are all of these synchronicities that convince you that life is magically perfect. More importantly when the heart opens you are able to make decisions from a place of love, instead of fear.

Are you willing to learn to cultivate an ability to operate from a place of 'in love' all of the time? Is that possible? Yes, it is. Does it require discipline, faith, persistence, and healing? Yes, it most definitely does! To heal any addiction to fear and negativity ultimately frees you of karma. In the habit of negativity there is very little memory about who you really are, rather the brain and ego are running rampant pushing adrenaline through your experience of all the ways you are not safe, not loveable, not worth it. Let me tell you right now —you are worth it! If you are engaged with this material you are ready to confront the truth about who you are, and you are ready to engage with and be guided by your intuition.

Intuition is something most of us have to reconnect to. We had it when we were young and it has to be awakened and developed. This happens by using it, not merely thinking about it. Intuition can be accessed in many unique ways, with each of these as individual and unique as you. Intuition takes openness, imagination, willingness, trust, expansion, faith, listening, feeling, seeing, and smelling. You may say, "Why imagination? You are just making it up if you are using your imagination." Imagination is the equalizing tool it takes to circumvent the rigidity of the brain. Imagination is the creativity container for the new, for change, and ultimately for the Universal Energy Flow. Imagination opens you up.

I am going to take you back to the beginning of the healing work and my early experiences doing the breathing exercise. The vibration of my energy turned on so strong it never fully receded back to what I was used to. By the third time I did the breathing in Sedona, Arizona with the mystic healer, Tim Heath, my energy turned on completely. I was vibrating 24-7, and it was so strong that I did not sleep much for the ten days I was there. I thought it was Sedona and the full moon, and then I learned it was not. Over time I grew to understand how my essence had merged into my body, and I became comfortable with its vibration. Twenty years later I am still vibrating.

I'm not telling this story for you to think that I'm special, I tell it because it has become the foundation of the healing work. I have been able to put enough pieces of the puzzle together for it to finally make more and more sense, and I hope I can share the significance of it with you. I believe we are constantly vibrating and pulsing with energy through the nervous system. However, the brain and ego dominate the conscious state so much that this connection is not perceived or developed on the physical level. The breath work fine-tunes the connection between your body and the frequency of your soul; once you feel this consistently enough it starts to become your foremost communication system.

This awareness becomes the foundation of the intuition, which becomes its own language of connection to the Universe and the world of the spirit. It is an experience that becomes one prolonged goose bump, a measurement of truth that actually allows the brain to take a well-deserved rest. Once the connection is made to your essence and it is allowed to merge into your physical body, all of your experiences of life take on a whole new meaning. You experience them as feelings, as energy, as sound, as light, as smell, and ultimately as love. Once you move into this realm it becomes clear how everything is connected and flows together in harmony as a Universal expression of love.

Okay, it took me many years to figure this out. I am willing to help you through this process at your own pace. The starting point is to develop your awareness with the energy of your essence. The breath is the key to initiate this connection and fine-tune your awareness to your soul. Once you develop yourself in this arena, and connect the dots around the Power of Love, you are on your way. Your soul is a Universal vibration of love. As I said in the beginning of the book, most people do not develop the discipline around getting to know their own essence. It is too much effort. Nevertheless, if you do this work you will complete your karma for this life and along the way you may just help many others, which will make you happy.

Once you can experience your soul vibration and learn to be guided by it as energy then it becomes the tool for your intuition to grow. Intuition is a craft that is developed. In most cases it is not a privileged gift. It is a developed gift. The same is true of faith; you are not born with it as much as you cultivate it over time. Whether it is faith or intuition, it is kind of like riding a bicycle; once you can stay on the bike you can begin to journey to many places.

In its purest form, intuition flows through your heart as a vibration of love from the Universe; when you can maintain neutrality, your essence then helps you understand the information and intuition becomes an empowering flow of Universal Energy. Without neutrality many people base their intuition on a volatile emotional frequency calibrated and made logical through the ego-controlled brain. This information is limited because it often has human investments in it; consequently, this frequency is not rooted through the soul. This way of working with intuition is tricky and most of the time steeped in superstition and negativity because it is based more in fear and a place of no self-love. It is controlled more through the human faculties of the emotions and mind. Even if the information has a psychic energy to it, chances are it will be negative. An example of this is given in the chapter of Being Extreme (p. 53), where someone can be marketed to in the places where they do not love themselves.

Not to ruffle too many feathers for people who work this way, but if you do, check in and see how much personal energy you use trying to do your work. It can end up draining the life force because the brain and emotions do not allow the same access to the Universal Energy Flow. If you are reading here then I assume you are open to be working with the Universal Energy Flow. It will prove to energize you endlessly.

Here's how I've come to understand my own experience with my intuition as it developed.

When I first started doing healing work my intuition would come in a few different ways. I would get goose bumps, or pulses of energy when I would hear or feel the truth. That was my primary awakener signifying I was in the presence of something greater than me. Then I started to recognize that the goose bumps would show up in different ways on and through my body. If it were something I spoke and felt, I would get the goose bumps on my arms. If it were something I heard or felt when someone else was speaking, I would feel them across my shoulders. If it were a truth with a deep emo-

tional energy to it I would feel the energy move from the second chakra up my spine.

Notice I am not saying I felt any goose bumps around what I was 'seeing', nevertheless, as I paid attention and realized when my heart was open—as signified by the goose bumps around my hearing (truth) and feeling (heart opening to love) some energy would start to move around my third eye—seeing. Through my conscious awareness of when my heart was open, I started to receive intuition around my vision. The more awareness I brought to the distinction of what was happening, the more the energy/intuition would flow.

As this began to make sense something really exciting started to happen! Just as I would get goose bumps, a red-tailed hawk would fly over and scream. This started to happen every time, and it became an external non-human validation for 'the intuition.' Notice the distinction now. I started to realize that the intuition was coming from somewhere else. I was just the receptor and conduit. It really was not mine, but for the sake of communicating in this section I will continue to call it mine. I got the message from the Universe and I let go of ownership! I was then able to allow the red-tailed hawk to become a powerful alliance helping me trust the Universal Energy Flow as it moved through me in the form of goose bumps. This always followed a feeling of supreme truth. Are you with me?

Then I started to track through my awareness an intuition of the hawk presence before I would hear or see it, sometimes even prior to getting the goose bumps. I would take it all in. Gradually I realized the events around my intuition were connected. Then other scenarios came into play such as when a hawk would show up and land, and when they would continue to circle and scream for many minutes. I realized that each circumstance had its own meaning, it was a clear communication from the Universe. It is amazing what you can learn if you just pay attention!

As these connectors to my intuition grew I was allowed to become more and more neutral to the other person's experience. I was able to be detached and hold space for the person from a place of love. Simultaneously their experience became more and more profound for them. Truth would permeate every cell of their body. I realized as the conduit, whatever I was feeling they were feeling, too. They would be feeling the goose bumps; they would hear the hawks just as intensely as I would. The experience was Universal for those in the moment with me, whether with one other person or a group of people.

My intuition continued to grow. I was able to connect more dots about the power of the emotions for healing when the Universal Energy Flow moves them. The goose bumps or hawk were the signifier, letting me know that in these instances the brain did not drive the emotions. Much of this early development happened while I was in the middle of a healing session, which only heightened my awareness to the whole intuitive process I call healing. I was aware there were many tools contributing to the opening including: the breath, essential oils, music, sage, etc. I had to factor all of these things into the curriculum as the Universe worked to help me trust and reconnect to my intuition so that I could learn how to do the work effortlessly. This development taught me that the work was not about me, it was about opening myself up to be guided by the Universe through my intuition.

Many other layers of intuition continued to build the more I worked. Strong connection happened with the elements, especially the wind. I started to feel a gentle breeze just as a hawk would fly over, this would also intensify the energy with the goose bumps. Sometimes the breeze would be very strong, always getting my attention and announcing it was another player in the game. From there I started to feel stronger manifestations in my body with sensations. After the moment of truth, the goose bumps, the hawk, and the wind, I often would feel energy move through my heart. In the same moment people in my presence would generally open their hearts and let go of their pent-up emotions.

Sometimes their body would convulse with spirit moving through it. Their body temperature would begin to get much hotter. I would usually say, "The Holy Spirit is hot!" I would feel the heat moving through the other person. The heat would have its own information for me. Oftentimes I would feel this in the base of my spine. Then I would witness hummingbirds dancing in front of my face; sometimes they would come into my workspace, or flutter and dart about just outside the window. The energy would stimulate a warm fuzzy vibration of love through my heart. At this point in the experience everything would start to remind me of old Walt Disney movies. Animals in all forms—crows, squirrels, owls, bobcats, butterflies, my dog Buffy—would start to dance and come closer. It was a realization that tickled my fancy. I love nature! I realized nature loves the vibration of love, joy, and peace. And this was a confirmation that healing was bigger, more connected, and easier than I ever imagined.

I found that intuition is a primary tool that allows me

to connect to the Universe and that it can provide guidance,
support and possibility. As I learned to exchange with the
Universe through my conscious awareness, my intuition de-
veloped accordingly. It is truly all connected!

I am not going to suggest your experience has to be anything like mine. However, I have seen many others open to
their intuition, why not give it a try?

Exercise 15 is a very important one for you to pay attention to. I would love for you to work with it for six months.
Pay attention! **Where awareness goes, energy flows.** As you
give this exercise awareness your intuition will awaken, the
Universe will feed you with validation, you will start to have
a lot of fun paying attention and getting connected to the
moment. And most of all your intuition will grow, bringing
you a greater sense of freedom, enlightenment, and empow-
erment. Enjoy!

INTUITION – PART 2

It is okay to move on to this section before you take six
months to do all of the work in Part 1. Use your discipline to
connect the dots with your intuition and you will not regret
it. This next section will take you much deeper; the stronger
your foundation from applying the prior intuition section, the
more connection to Universal Energy Flow you will have.

Someone asked me if intuition was just interesting and
beneficial to healers. I explained that in everything I do I
use my intuition—every step I take, every breath I make!
It would not be life without intuition. The farmer uses intuition every day with crops and animals; the hunter uses
intuition when hunting wildlife; the midwife uses intuition

Intuition ⸱ Exercise 15

1. Develop a relationship with the pranayama breath work mentioned throughout the book. It is a fundamental tool in this work (see p. 48).

2. Develop your connection to your soul through the experience with the breath. Start to make notes of how the Universe communicates to you through your energy (e.g. I tingle and vibrate around my mouth, my hands get hot, I release stuck emotions, etc.). This is the key to developing your intuition.

3. Do you already have some guides and alliances that help you with your intuition? Try to list everything that comes to you in conjunction with your intuition. Put down everything you have memory of, and everything you are experiencing doing the breath work.

4. Take another sheet of paper and start to connect the dots, try to track your intuition in the general way that it communicates to you (e.g. truth, goose bumps, hawks, wind, heat, hummingbirds, warm fuzzy feeling in the heart—love, an awareness of Universal Energy Flow, the response of animals).

when helping deliver a baby; the tennis player uses intuition when playing a tennis game; the taxi driver uses intuition to drive safely through traffic, etc. Intuition is a part of life no matter what you do, and no matter how much you embrace or deny it.

Rachel, a young scientist, age 32, came to me stating she had used math to make her way to the top of her profession. She was considered one of the brightest minds in her field, however she could not for the life of her figure out men and relationships. The guys she attracted were cold, unemotional, and in their heads. I tried my best not to tease her, but of course asked her just how smart she was? She looked at the ceiling. I started reminding her that every time she looked up, she was going to her brain for the answers (Generally when someone looks up they are looking to the brain, when they look down, they look to the emotions in the belly).

Eventually she gave in and said she was feeling like she needed a new approach to attract a mate. I said, "Feeling is good!" I asked her to describe her future partner. She looked at the ceiling, she stopped herself and we smiled at each other. She instinctively looked down. She was smart! She connected to her feelings and proceeded to use her intuition to describe the man she ended up with. It took her about six months to run this program, and she showed amazing aptitude with her intuition. I believe incredibly bright people have just as much intuition as anyone else; they just have to be willing to use it. In these six months she committed to doing the seven-minute meditation every day, and to visualize the partner she described to me in the session. The exercise of using her imagination to see her partner in her mind ended up being a lot of fun for Rachel. She was quite proud when she brought her partner in to meet me.

I smile when people commit to doing the work, and create the experience they are looking for.

The next level of growth with your intuition takes awareness, attention, neutrality, focus, practice, trust, ethics, boundaries, faith, more practice, discipline, and more practice! This next level takes the work into the psychic realm with intuition. If you are invested in fear or insecurity and not clean, clear, and intuitively aligned with the Universe this level will not be accessible to you for a sustained period of time. You will burn out, it will dry up, and you will lapse back into your old reality. Allow me to explain. Being in alignment with the Universe will push you, developing your intuition will push you, cleaning up your ethics to be on purpose with your walk and talk will definitely push you! So, know what you are getting yourself into because sometimes it is easier to be half-asleep.

If you are ready to be clear, to be operating on a fully aware and intuitive level—you will have to do some work. I know a lot of highly intuitive people, however most are not developed around the power of their intuition because they have not done the work on themselves.

Their frailties include being ungrounded, flighty, and too fragile on an emotional level because they are too invested in fear. They have high receptivity with their intuition; however, they do not have enough discipline around trusting themselves so it can fully develop. This is the case with most of the empathic people I meet; they are too frail to be accountable during most activities. They usually do not do well with groups, especially large groups, and they are highly reactive to certain kinds of people. They are chemically sensitive, air sensitive, food sensitive, sensitive to cities, sensitive to pollen, sensitive to dust, pollution, etc. If fear has shut them down, how can their intuition be of service to them? And to drive this point home—most highly sensitive people thrive on this attention. It gives them a right to be fanatical, or extreme.

For your intuition to develop and strengthen it has to be allowed to protect and guide you when you're faced with challenges. The times when the brain is screaming to take control are the times when intuition is needed the most. This is why one needs to learn to tap into the Universal Energy Flow, which will keep you clear and energized.

Intuition thrives on love, faith, peace, grace, nature, and freedom.

Developing your intuition is the key to freedom. When I talk about this level most people gloss over and stare blankly at me. It has taken me many years to hone and craft this area to a workable art form; I hope to convey this to you now. See, hear, and feel the intention of my communication! You can do it!

At its highest level your intuition is operating on spiritual/psychic realms (I use the words spiritual and psychic interchangeably as long as the psychic realm is focused into the light for the positive benefit of all). If you can trust your intuition on this level it can pave the way for ease on the mental, emotional, and physical levels. If you can head the negative thoughts and energies off in the spiritual level, then you do not have to deal with them on the others.

For instance, if I happen to think of someone—seemingly random—I pay attention right away. I do not disregard it. I make it a point to deal with what I feel, hear, or see in that moment with the person I thought of. Say I think of my friend Rob. I first sense what the energy feels like. Does it lift me up and does it feel like love? If it does, I will welcome it, acknowledge it, and return the feeling. I may say, "Hey Rob, what's going on?" I will listen and engage for a split second with my intuition and return an exchange of energy. Most of the time I do this quietly within my consciousness and sometimes I will speak aloud. If the initial feeling is negative I will say, "No, not welcome! Stop." Then I will block the energy from taking hold within my consciousness and return to the commitment to keep my heart open and keep myself clear. If I sense upset somewhere with that person, and if I know what it is about, I will answer psychically, set a boundary, or send a communication by phone or email that will handle it.

Most of the time a psychic communication will handle most energetic inquiries that come to me through my intuition. If I ignore my intuition and do not head things off at the pass—close to when they are occurring within another person—then I can expect things to become more confronting for me later. I can expect the incident to materialize into something that will take more energy on the mental, emotional, or physical levels. Who wants that to occur?

INTUITION: PART 2 ⸱ EXERCISE 16

Start to work with your awareness to develop these skills.

1. Every time you think of someone ask yourself, "Is this my thought or theirs? Am I generating it? Or are they?" If they keep 'randomly' popping into your mind it is usually their thoughts. You have to be clear here! You may not always know at first but be easy about it. If you engage with this your intuition will grow.

2. If it is your thought/energy ask yourself, "What do I want from them?" And proceed from there. You have to deal with you and take responsibility for your thoughts and feelings. Clean them up when necessary.

3. If it is their thought/energy ask yourself, "Does this feel like love? Does it lift me up? Is the vibration expansive?"

4. If it feels like love you can let it in and send love back. This is a circle. It will energize you and make you happy. This adds energy to the Universe and brings grace flowing back to you.

5. If it does not feel like love this is where the work
    and boundary development comes in. This is where
    clarity with your intuition is imperative! This is
    where you say "No!" to the thought/energy. Not
    welcome. You do not have to go to war. You can be
    gentle, but you must be firm. Most people do not
    expect to be handled on the psychic/spiritual plane.
    Most are not even conscious that their thoughts
    and feelings can be felt on this level.

6. When you say an energetic 'no' notice how many
    more times you have to say it. This will teach you
    how much work you have to do to strengthen your
    boundaries, and it will teach you about the energies
    you have aligned with to learn your lessons.

7. When one 'no' consistently handles these situations
    you will have reached a place of awareness where
    you can start to deal with your essence and true
    purpose in life. In other words the channels will be
    open enough, and you will be in touch with your
    intuition to be guided to remember who you are.
    From there it becomes a treasure hunt following
    spirit and its divine plan for your existence. Hal-
    lelujah! This is what most of us are searching for.

INTUITION SUMMARY

At the beginning of the book I wrote: ...most humans are underdeveloped spiritually; underdeveloped because most have little consciousness or spiritual discipline in their life. A small percentage of humans are willing to connect the dots and see how X on a spiritual level affects things created on physical, emotional, and mental levels. This is what this work is about as we look at everything from the cause and effect of the spiritual plane.

This is the work with your intuition I am talking about. You have to develop yourself to be accountable to you and your connection to the Universe. You are guided at all times.

If you want freedom in your life—including freedom from stress, anxiety and worry—develop your intuition. The net result is your intuition will connect you to the Universe, and the Universe will become your guide and employer. You will feel encouraged and supported to be operating from an amazingly stress-free place of light and inspiration. As long as your intuition is connected to the Universal Energy Flow it will not drain or exhaust you. It is a renewable energy source and it is free! The only investment it requires from you is your awareness and discipline to cultivate it.

Do the work, pay attention to the signs—they are everywhere! Once you grow confidence with your intuition nothing can take it away. It is a beautiful garden! And you do not have to call yourself a healer at all; it is fine if you call yourself a wife, husband, teacher, lawyer, writer, doctor, student, child. Now, go travel in the light!

Healer Training students of all ages have shown tremendous ability to identify guides, alliances, and spirits that help with their intuition. I have seen clients and students rapidly develop the gift of clairaudience in particular, and I am happy to see and hear of their results. The people with the biggest appetites, who follow through doing the work, have turned into amazing healers. Even those who have faced the biggest hurdles or have the lowest self-esteem have become powerful healers. I am very pleased to have played a small role in their development!

As I said earlier it takes discipline to develop on the spiritual path. Impress yourself with your ability to be disciplined. Develop yourself beyond your default tendencies. Be honest about your basic limitations and grow in the areas where you want to experience more. The journey can be slow and confronting—and it is worth every second of your effort. When it gets gritty, check in, you may want to take a step back and have gratitude for your growth. Stick with it. Do the work. Do not avoid changing the less attractive, stuck or aggressive aspects of your behavior. Your love and respect for yourself will only grow, and you will be amazed by how this enriches your creativity.

CREATIVITY

Creativity is the tool for forward movement through your pain, through the past, and through to the other side of freedom. Most people I come into contact with have a basic need to express themselves; to speak up, and to be seen and heard. Some of the most successful growth and healing that I have witnessed has happened through the use of creativity. Creativity is another way to access Universal Energy Flow. Creativity takes a person choosing to express him or herself, and puts them in relationship with the Universe. It lets them heal and help others through their expression. It is a direct route to healing, love, exchange, grace, Universal Energy Flow, and freedom.

Over the years I have said many times, "How you do anything is how you do everything." If a person has something to express and they are waiting, or avoiding the risk of expression, I have found this can make them sick. I decided long ago to help people heal by getting them on purpose with expression in their life. I would tell myself, "Why not direct the work to set people free through creation?" It has made the work far more interesting to me because it has forward movement to it. Creative expression empowers people, energizes them and fills them with spirit. Once they are turned on by spirit, anything and everything they do will magically fall into place and feel full.

When I realized there was a plan for me to work with artists in Hollywood I became aware how much of a sense of humor the Universe has. It put me in Hollywood pursuing an acting career for several years, and it taught me about the life of the artist. As I finally accepted life as a healer, I realized I was still an artist. The way I look at it, everything is art, and everything I do is art. Healing is an art form. Therefore, I have spent over half my life as an artist (acting and healing). I realized all the areas where I had withheld my expression always came from the same place, or story of, "I do not feel safe. I cannot open up. They do not get me."

The 'story' always comes back to the same starting point:

- I was not loved the right way

- I was not loved enough
- I was not loved at all
- I am not loveable
- Why?

For the sake of this discussion I no longer care about why. I care about this:

*I have something to do here. Let's go. Let me get on with my work, my art, my creativity, my mission, and my purpose. All the things that have happened to me in my life are my assets. They are what makes me, me. I am willing to take full responsibility for everything that has ever happened to me. I attracted it for the **experience and lesson** that I needed to learn about love. I am loveable. I deserve love from others, because I love and respect myself. I know who I am, and what I stand for. I am willing to express myself fully—now. It is my time to risk sharing what I have learned.*

It is probable that there are others out there who feel the same way, and it is probable that they are feeling the urgency to step forward and claim their right to be present here on the planet in this time of change and opportunity. What better way to step forward than to be using creativity, writing, and full expression? As creative artists we have a refinement to who we are, we are very sensitive sentient beings who live and thrive on love. Let us go forth and sow the seeds of freedom and equality expressed as love. Let us risk sharing the depths of how we feel about peace, harmony, and guardianship for the Mother Earth. Let us not fear departure from many of the negative ways of our culture. Let us be willing to step forth and share with people through our expression – our stories, movies, music, art, pottery, jewelry, books, dance, etc. Let us attract like souls who love to play and celebrate healing and all things around us through our conscious choice to create. We are all creators, and with the Creator's help we can bring peace and harmony to this planet.

This is how I feel. I know creative expression is the way. I know it contains the dance of attraction, and within these intentional magnetisms love can be expressed as a force to illuminate the way for others who choose to travel up this road with us. I am not saying you have to quit your job, change careers or find an agent and get headshots, rather I am saying see your life as art. Express your heart through your art. As I am writing this and making these choices to express this to you the Universe around me starts to dance with life. Ravens caw, hummingbirds dart in front of me, my kitty purrs, a ground squirrel calls from its den. The Universe, love, and my creativity are all one and the same. They flow from the same source.

Let me just say it here and now. Creativity is the shortcut to healing! When creative people come in to see me and tell me how negative they are acting in their life, the easiest recommendation I have for them is, "Get back to creating!" Results happen so fast oftentimes I do not hear from them again for years.

CREATIVITY ⚜ EXERCISE 17

1. Write down the types of creativity you are sitting on, doubting, suppressing or resisting within. If you are frustrated, depressed or in a negative relationship in any aspect of your life then you are squelching your expression. The exchange between you and the Universe is off. It is time to love yourself, exchange with the Universe and set your creativity free.

2. Pick an art form—writing, singing, painting or dance—and unleash your creative expression with it. Exchange with your creativity, love it, embrace it! Use it to set yourself free. When you become excited about your life because of your creative expression everything magically falls into place.

3. Make a commitment to express your creativity on a consistent basis. As you do this your confidence will grow. Take risks to express yourself. Give birth. Let yourself become excited and play! Dare to experiment.

If you have been pregnant with creativity for most of your life—consider a woman in the last weeks of pregnancy. Listen to how uncomfortable she can become waiting for this baby to emerge. Her body aches and screams. What is your body telling you? What is it you need to give birth to? It is the same feeling for a man or a woman. If you are sitting on your creativity and not doing what you karmically signed on to do then the Universe is going to push you. The discomfort is only going to get worse.

If you can hear what I am saying then I am talking to you. If you are stuck, frustrated and pregnant with creativity, you may need to change your life. You may just need to get out the guitar and play or write in a journal. Be honest with yourself and honor your creative expression. When you do this you will start to experience peace, love, laughter, healing, and freedom. Let's go!

> *Susan, a 47 year-old client, finally decided to give writing a try in her life. She had been a wife, a corporate exec, an entrepreneur, and nothing had clicked. She felt frustrated! She always thought about writing, but could never get past her judgment that writing was not a career. I sensed her talent for writing for years; while every one of our sessions had focused on her marriage, corporate life and small business ventures, they always came back to her ideas about writing.*
>
> *Eventually Susan realized she was not happy doing the things she was doing, and she decided to tell her story. She never lacked for stories, and she had a flair for sharing them. Through this expressive art form she found healing. As her self-esteem grew, more people gathered round to hear her perspective on life. Using her creativity to express her talent set her free. It became contagious! The next thing I knew she was writing books on women's healing and self-empowerment. She found the love inside herself that she was always looking for. She fulfilled her destiny and in some ways she's just getting started.*

RESISTANCE, AVOIDANCE, AND LACK OF CONFIDENCE WITH CREATIVITY

How much do these words define your experience of life? Is it a constant battle to overcome resistance? Is avoiding something easier than dealing with it? Do you feel you have the potential to contribute to society in a meaningful way, but lack the confidence to try? Why play the game of suppressing yourself any longer?

Suppression can be defined as repression, shut down, hush-up, control and prevention by force. Where does it come from? Does it come from outside of you (e.g. a critical parent, teacher, partner or friend)? Or does suppression truly reside deep inside of you? Do you suppress yourself and kill off your creativity to remain invisible and small? In the section before, I explained about my choice to see myself as an artist all of the time. I suspect you are an artist, too. What role does resistance, avoidance, and lack of confidence play in your life? Does it push you even when you do not want to deal with it? Is being an artist part of your karmic path? Does this path keep presenting you with opportunities to step up to the artistic plate? Are you going to become accountable for who you really are? Or are you going to blame others for the lack of safety you feel?

If you are waiting for it to feel safe you might as well Velcro the remote to your hand and order another bottle of vodka. Creative expression is not going to feel safe to the unexercised, underdeveloped side of your true self, especially with an overdeveloped ego reminding you how easy it is to resist, avoid, and remain invisible. Let me say it another way; creative expression is not going to feel safe if you do not love yourself.

If you have lacked the confidence to live up to your potential it is because you are not loving you. Why not love yourself and try to express your creativity now? Think about the wonderful flow of energy that could move through you when you trust creativity and love yourself. How it expands, recharges, and fills you with spirit and life force energy. Why would you resist this feeling? Even better, maybe it is time to realize that accepting, engaging, and expressing yourself is the shortcut to your spiritual development this lifetime. Step into it, work through the fear of being seen and heard for the creativity spiraling out of your heart.

The one area in life where I believe fear takes you to a spiritual experience is in art, expression and creativity. Creative risk activates your energy so intensely it is like doing the breathing meditation. The key is to use the heightened energy, which opens you up. Let go of control and sing through your throat chakra—even if you're off key, feel through the heart—even if the feeling is fear, and see through the third eye—even if your vision is blurry; your vibration will rise and, before you know it, your spirit will join you in your body as you step though fear and choose to express.

I once had an acting teacher tell me to 'out-create' the fear, judgment and self-criticism by choosing to take action and create. When we choose to use our talent and trust it to get us into unknown territories where our mind is not in control, then we find the freedom creativity offers. The more you do this, the more your confidence in the creative process grows. Experience is a great teacher!

My first film acting close up showed me why actors act. I literally felt my chakras start to spin in my base and the feel-

ing moved up my spine. When the energy got to my throat I could not speak. That's the beauty of the film camera close-up, I did not need to, and by the time I could speak, the communication that needed to happen on film had happened. It was a magical feeling and I have never forgotten it.

There are times when I am writing when I feel the same activation. However, the strongest it usually occurs is when I have the most to risk publicly. That's when my talent has its biggest opportunity to shine and my mind and ego can make me feel the most vulnerable. I have learned these are the moments to seize. To say, "Yes!" and step over the line of doubt. Through trusting the Universe to support me with love, I feel an unbelievable exchange of energy flow through me whether I am acting, leading a breathing circle, teaching a class, or sharing this book. I have learned to reframe my understanding of the energy of fear and shift it to excitement. This is the spiritual moment that happens with creative expression. When I choose to risk is when the energy transforms from fear (contraction) to excitement (expansion). This is when my uniqueness is revealed. I have learned that the moment of 'risking' is when I feel goose bumps and it is when others connect to me the most. This is the place when I know I am connected to my intuition and I feel the Universal Energy Flowing through me.

When I speak in front of large groups I tell people about my experience in that moment. I explain how my gift of hearing works and that my clairaudience is allowing me to hear more than what's being spoken. I also share about how strongly I am vibrating and how the energy feels. As I do this, I see people settle down and start to vibrate with me instead

*of feeling uncomfortable from too much energy in the room
that is not being referenced or talked about. If I am leading
a group it is up to me to clarify what is going on in the room.
If I am using my creative gifts to explain what is happening
it expands and teaches people at the same time. This is how
I deal with highly creative moments in my life and how I
make them positive experiences for me as opposed to resisting
or avoiding them. Through this example I am encouraging
you to risk, share, and let people into your process. The very
thing you feel most vulnerable and insecure about will end
up being your biggest asset and will make you more human
to others.*

CREATIVITY MEDITATION
EXERCISE 18

If you have a recorder, record this next section and use
it in a meditation. I suggest doing ten minutes of the
pranayama breathing and as you start to open and vibrate play this message that came through the 'voice'
that guides me. There is an energy you can access
through these words. I feel the energy when it comes
through and I relay the message to you.

*Who are you? Why are you here in this body this lifetime?
Are you here to play the game or are you here to watch the
game? If you know there is more to life than what you have
been experiencing, if you have always felt this – then it is
time to wake up. As I mentioned earlier it may be easier to*

remain asleep. At first it will be confronting to see, hear, and feel through the illusion that most humans live by, nevertheless, if you are able to hear this message it is meant for you. Most will pass it by; such is existence here on the true mother ship, Mother Earth.

If you can hear the message, and you have accumulated a wealth of training, knowledge, and information to share, it is time for you to awaken to your purpose. You are a messenger for the higher dimensional beings that work through the physical realms here on Earth. These beings have an allegiance to humans that is not based on our prior actions, but based more on our innate potential to love and be loved.

The Power of Love is vast beyond measure. It is beyond science and beyond intellect. It is a power that ignites the human spirit, and flows as light connecting us to all things – as One. We have underachieved with our potential to love and be connected to all things. We have isolated ourselves as 'the one, the superior, the dominant' power, disconnecting ourselves from all of the things that give us existence and life: namely the Earth, sun, stars, moon, sky, water, air, fire, nature – the Universal Energy Flow! We have been seduced by the Love of Power, which gets us nowhere.

The higher dimensional beings, call them God, angels, deities, spirits, masters, or light are choosing to get our attention now. They are calling forth the contracts signed long ago; for many the time of amnesia is over. If you know you are a messenger with a message to deliver, you will have to be the conduit for it soon, otherwise your contract will be taken over by another who will deliver the message, leaving you with a familiar empty feeling. If you know this feeling and you do *not like it—get creating now! As you birth the message, those meant to engage with it will find it. Do not worry about the logistics. The higher energies will be your representative, your agent, your curator, your publisher and teammate. Let's go!*

CREATIVITY: CHALLENGE
EXERCISE 19

1. Take a big risk; tell your best friend you are going to start a creative project you have been waiting to do your whole life. For some of you it might be to write your book, for others it may be to buy a guitar and start taking lessons, for another it may be to work with watercolors, or for someone else it might be to simply write a poem. Let your heart guide you in taking this risk, it is not about your mind.

2. Share your risk with a family member.

3. Tell a complete stranger: "Got a new guitar today!" "I'm going to paint." "I'm writing poetry."

By the time you repeat the story three times the Universe will hear you. Notice your energy as you start to get excited. Have fun with the process, see what happens, and let me know how it goes.

Writing has been my biggest creative risk so far and I am a changed person for doing it. I cannot encourage you enough to use your creativity. I knew there was something to using my throat in acting and letting a character come through, but that pales in comparison to what I have experienced as a writer.

WRITING AS HEALING

Writing is a powerful tool for healing yourself and others. There can be a lot of resistance to the creative process with writing. It forces you to use many of your abilities such as intellect, creativity, intuition, humor, and discipline. The experience of writing my first book and now this one has proven to be very challenging and enlightening for me. It has been challenging in my doubtful moments to trust that these words could really help someone, and it has been incredibly enlightening as I feel the Universe nudging me on. When I am in the creative process of writing, my life becomes even more magical than it already is.

I believe the power of the writing process is one of the reasons people have so much resistance to writing. 'What if' you influenced one person in a positive way with your writing? 'What if' you influenced millions of people with your writing? 'What if' you trusted yourself to express beyond your ability to know the outcome of the message the Universe was giving you? Would you be a messenger then?

Let's stop here before we go too far into the big picture, and let's get back to you. Let us peer into the mirror and see how writing can benefit where you are in your life. The deeper you expose your experience, the more others can relate to you. But more importantly—early on in your writing—the deeper you go into your experience, the more you open, the more you share—the more you will see into the mirror of yourself. The more intimacy you will have with you. Now, this is not to say all writing needs to be deep and serious. Humor is one of the great art forms available to the writer. There are many ways of expressing yourself and getting your point across.

But 'what if?' What if you expressed yourself enough to get beyond all the resistance and limitation that has been in your way of feeling and thinking about yourself? What if you trusted yourself to be the messenger to you? What if you felt, listened, and wrote to your heart's content? What if you became content in your life? What if you became content with you? How much better of a place would the world become? And from this place could you be the mustard seed for others? Could you start to reach deeper into the Universal pool of consciousness and touch others with the message? Has the Universe been whispering in your ear for some time now, "Let's go."

I remember reading and doing all of the exercises in The Artist's Way *by Julia Cameron when it first came out. It helped move some energy in me at the time and it made me start dealing with myself as an artist. The more I look at myself as an artist the more I have to listen to my heart and find the truth in my life so that I can express from that place.*

FINDING TRUTH INSIDE

I have found the more I have worked with my intuition and creativity, the better my sense of knowing what is going on around me, and the world at large. I rely on my intuition to guide me, and interestingly enough, I use my creativity to interpret all the signals I am receiving. The mixture becomes a dowsing rod for how I live and express my life. I am aware that I need all of the intuition I can muster to stay clear in these fluctuating times we are living in. It seems that the status of truth on the planet is foggy at best. I cannot help but feel that there is something going on with governments, politicians, banks, corporations, oil companies, and big business to name a few. So what is the truth? Do you wonder about this?

My intuition helps me recognize as much as I can take in and filter through. I have always wanted to know the truth. I incarnated this lifetime seeking the truth. The more work I do, the more I realize the spiritual responsibility that comes with the development of myself as a leader. As this happens, the realization becomes clear that spiritual freedom comes from extending a hand to help others along the path to peace, harmony, and well-being. It comes from the willingness to share what I have learned through the use of my intuition and creativity into the healing work, teaching, and writing.

It is important to develop yourself intuitively to know the truth in any situation. To know when you are in the presence of truth by the way it stimulates your spirit to move through you. The quandary is just how finely tuned can you be and remain functional in today's world? You do not have to be a Sensitive who resonates with spirit to know there are distortions in many areas of life where there is a Love of Power such as big business, government and politics.

We cannot complain, shut down, numb ourselves, or ignore situations that are not right in the world. How do you function in the world and not be affected by it? How do you spiritually use these times to empower yourself and the people around you? I do not think it is about the conspiracy of it all, and even if there were a huge conspiracy it would just be an opportunity for us to wake up. Each and every one of us has to be able to get to the truth in as many situations in our life as possible, and be willing to take a peaceful stand for what we know to be right, fair, and just to all involved.

How do we, the common people get heard? We have to be willing to stand for what we believe in politics and beyond. We have to be our own politician. The choice to spiritually connect to the truth is the first step. When we resonate with that truth others can feel into it. This is our responsibility as healers. From there our ability to love, share, teach, create, and exchange with others about how to open to their spirit and to help them to find their way is the catalyst for change.

FINDING TRUTH INSIDE
MEDITATION ⸱ EXERCISE 20

If you are concerned with the world picture, the financial times, politics, environment, war, as well as peace, family and raising kids, then you benefit by cultivating your intuition to the point where it can be your inner compass:

1. Lie down.

2. Do the breathing meditation, or another meditation you like to get yourself to an open, neutral place (refer to p. 48).

3. When you are vibrating, ask your intuition to guide and work with you.

4. Pick one topic you would like guidance on (e.g. environment, family issue, relationship, politics, etc.).

5. Ask your intuition to show you the truth about the topic you chose. Let it come to you, you may see it, hear it, or feel it. Notice the sensation and the experience that comes to you. Relax and enjoy the truth.

section three

HEALING YOURSELF

Healing Yourself

PERSONAL HEALING

Next we will delve deeper into ways to heal yourself. I know some of you have jumped ahead to this section. It is okay, though I encourage you to start back at the beginning of the book and do all of the exercises, they will help you connect all the dots.

I repeat, do the work. If you know there are problems. If you feel stuck, angry, sad or fearful, address the issue.

I think of John, a good friend's father, who was a chain smoker and a heavy drinker all of his adult life. When he was fifty-one, he was diagnosed with throat cancer. Big surprise? Of course we thought he would quit smoking and drinking. Not a chance. It was like one of those bad ads on TV. He kept smoking while wearing a radiation collar. Nobody expected him to recover, but he did. The cancer would reappear every 3-4 years, and he would get another collar and go through the same routine. He would say, you cannot teach an old dog new tricks. Finally, when he hit age 69, he got the worst news to date; the cancer was in his lungs. He did chemo and more radiation, all while smoking. It was sad to watch. The choice and chance to heal happened a long time before the cancer moved to his lungs. His wakeup call was in his earlier days.

I make strong suggestions for people facing disease and chronic illness to open up and address the call of their spirit. The Universe will communicate to you in your own language; if the communication has to manifest in the body to get your attention, you can bet the signals have been ignored for years. The process of taking medication to dampen the symptoms can delay this communication even further. Medication is a short-term fix because it doesn't address the cause of the illness. The illness is the invitation to open awareness to something deeper on the spiritual level. We have the capability to heal ourselves if we deal with the spiritual imbalance.

Below are some of the topics that we will cover in this section. I have picked these as some examples of the problems facing modern society. I am hoping you find the through line of healing and apply it to your situation:

- Sexual Abuse
- Cancer
- Marriage and Divorce
- Relationship
- Leadership Roles
- Money

As I say in the introduction, if you got yourself into this mess, I imagine you have some idea how to get yourself out. Review any of the exercises in the earlier chapters that were difficult; they are the areas where the compass keeps pointing. I can bet you ahead of time they will all come back to love and exchange. Is it really so simple? Am I going to target everything back to love? Pretty much. Review the diagram below and see where you stand with self-love or no self-love.

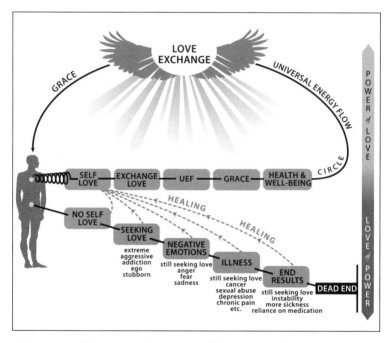

Diagram 9 – Self-Love as a Circle versus No Self-Love as a Dead End

SEXUAL ABUSE

Sexual abuse is one of the least understood, most ignored maladies facing humanity. It is a real problem, and in its most complex form it is a spiritual scourge that society has yet to fully deal with, or bring healing to in any significant way. In its most simple form it is a cry for love. Some of the questions about sexual abuse I continually look at are:

- ◆ What is the best way to bring attention and healing to this problem?

- ◆ Why is it so polarizing for people to talk about and deal with?

- ◆ Why do people carry this abuse their whole lives and have such difficulty healing it?

The best way to bring attention and healing to this problem is to keep talking and writing about it. It is very challenging to write about because there seems to be a powerful energetic force holding it in place. I will describe how I see, hear, feel, and work with sexual abuse energy. I hope it can help bring clarity to your life.

* This section might be difficult to digest in one read. I suggest that if you get sleepy, foggy, irritated, or angry at any point, stop, take a few breaths, and go back to the area where you felt clear. Read forward from there. You will need to keep loving yourself and exchanging with this material and the Universe to allow healing on a spiritual level. I have put as much love and intention into writing this chapter as I possibly can at this time. I am holding a bright light over it, and I am ex-

changing for all I am worth as I write this and share it with you. What's more, my sense of humor is intact! Namaste'

Here are a few definitions I will use as I discuss Sexual Abuse:

Sexual energy – The energy that moves through the sexual regions of the body (2nd chakra), which can be expressed in positive as well as negative ways.

Sexual abuse – Abusing someone by luring him or her into an exchange of sexual energy without their full awareness, or against their will. This abuse can happen physically, emotionally, mentally, spiritually, and psychically.

Sexual abuse energy – The energy that is passed into the victim. This energy leaves an imprint that acts as an entity, re-stimulating the person time and time again on all levels, moving as a sexual energy, both consciously and unconsciously.

Entity - A negative thought form, or energy that disguises itself as the person or part of their personality. A parasite that feeds off the energy of a host be it a person, animal, or plant.

Physical sexual abuse – When someone is raped, molested, or experiences unwanted physical contact that is sexual in nature.

Psychic sexual abuse – When someone is sexually abused on an energetic level and there is no physical contact; generally this happens in the higher, more spiritual realms because it is disguised as love.

Seduction – The act of luring somebody into sex, leading them astray, and abusing them by doing this against their will, or conscious choice.

Predator – A person who specializes in taking other people's energy, especially through sexual energy. They are masterful at creating a connection that immediately feels safe, intimate, and trustworthy. They have hypnotic abilities and are able to psychically seduce an adult or child into thinking sexual energy is love.

Victim – Injured party, prey, helpless person. Most people display strong compassion for a victim.

SEXUAL ABUSE ⁓ EXERCISE 21

1. What is your definition of sexual abuse?

2. What do you first think of at the mention of sexual abuse?

3. What is your story around sexual abuse energy?

4. What stage are you at in the healing of this abuse?

5. Do you believe you can heal it?

If you have been abused you will think of your experience first, or possibly something you may have done to someone else. You might also have skipped forward to this section. You may want to sit down and get comfortable, it is my intention to guide you to as much healing as possible. If you did skip forward, I am going to encourage you to go back and read from the beginning of the book. You will need all of the information about loving yourself and exchanging with the Universal Energy Flow to get the complete understanding of how I am referencing sexual abuse energy.

Sexual abuse is a difficult topic to discuss and it is deeply polarizing for people to talk about openly because it affects so many. It also evokes deep feelings of shame and/or guilt, and carries a powerful sense of stigma and taboo for all affected by this type of abuse. It is easily misunderstood with many varied opinions as to what causes it. Sexual abuse is a problem in society that is not being fully healed. In most instances healing is based on what happened physically, which is only one part of the problem; therefore, much of the time other aspects of the incident are swept under the rug and not talked about at all.

I'm not saying I have all the answers, but I feel like the opportunity for deeper healing is upon us, and my belief is that the energetic focus needs to be on the spiritual level for this to occur. If sexual abuse energy has not been successfully confronted and healed, it is because it has not yet been clearly worked with spiritually. **Sexual abuse has not been confronted on the spiritual level.** Let's see if we can connect the dots for you so that you can deal with it on this plane. As a society, we can no longer let this situation not be dealt with. I use the quote below because it says it all.

"Injustice anywhere is a threat to justice everywhere."
—Martin Luther King, Jr.

Open your imagination to the information below. When information like this comes through, it comes directly from the 'voice' that guides me through my gift of hearing, or clairaudience. Try to feel the energy in it; there might be some healing for you.

> *I am not speaking about churches, or religion when I talk about healing on the spiritual level. I will not rule that out, but to the best of my knowledge it has not been dealt with there yet. Sexual abuse energy has not been exposed at its deepest root of existence within the human lineage in the Love of Power that took hold here long ago. The exact memories are not necessary to get the healing that is needed. Sexual abuse energy has to be cleared on the spiritual level with humanity, as well as individuals, for the energy to be healed and cleansed. We are waiting for this moment to be crystallized in human awareness, and there have been powers blocking this experience on very deep levels of consciousness exerting control over the human experience; however, the days are numbered and the time for the Power of Love to be brought forth is close at hand! Let us move forward and see what we can uncover.*

Go back and review your answers to Exercise 21. Is sexual abuse about being taken advantage of physically (e.g. rape, physical molestation) with the physical, emotional, and mental experiences that go along with it? Or is it more of what happens on the psychic level? They are both real experiences, and the former will get the most attention from society because it is something that physically happens and appears to be the most damaging. The deed is easier to pinpoint, and there would seem to be an obvious path to heal it because of what is known on the physical level—Who was involved? What happened? Where did it occur? How did it occur? What were the injuries?

As a society we deal with sexual abuse and sexual assault through various institutions that each work to bring healing to the physical, emotional, and mental levels. I know that the establishments, from police departments and hospitals (physical), to social workers and therapists (emotional), and the legal and psychiatric systems (mental) are doing their jobs to the best of their abilities to bring about healing. It is a complex process and there are many factors that determine the rights of all involved. Ideally it should always be in the cleanest, most effective way possible. Offenses are being watched and tracked more and more by society. In the U.S. a convicted offender will carry these marks for the rest of their days; therefore, the stakes are higher. However, there is more in the healing process that can be done.

To bring healing to sexual abuse we have to go beyond the trauma of forced physical contact. As horrible as these occurrences are, there are many levels and degrees of awareness around the energy, intention, and act of sexual abuse beyond the incident and aftermath of physical assault.

To try to get to the core of this on the spiritual plane, I want to deal with the energy that moves between people as sexual abuse energy.

For the rest of the discussion I am going to primarily be talking about the psychic/spiritual side of sexual abuse. I distinguish the difference between spiritual and psychic as:

Spiritual – Of the soul; sacred, divine, mystical, holy, saintly, the light.

Psychic – Spiritual, telepathic, supernatural, intuitive, extrasensory; not always of the light, can be positive or negative. In the positive sense it is a spiritual condition based in love, in the negative it is a condition that is based in fear or fantasy.

I want to look more deeply into understanding psychic sexual abuse energy and why it is so acutely pervasive within the human experience. What drives this energy to do what it does? I have watched it for close to twenty years now and have continuously heard people talk about how therapists, counselors, psychics, and healers have sensed sexual abuse and yet the person has no active memories of anything happening to them. In many cases the memories may be blocked as a self-defense mechanism, and if this is the case, what does this do to the person over time? At a certain point when events have to be dealt with, they start to come to the surface, whether through dreams, destructive behavior, or illness. To make matters more complicated, even if a person remembers the details around an incident, it may or may not help with the healing. Often it may keep the awareness in the physical, and not take it deeper. Whether remembered or not, we have to get into the causal motivation to help people clear the energy on the deepest, most potent levels, which is with the spirit.

It is tricky to work with, heal and bring awareness to sexual abuse because this energy penetrates the human psyche in the form of a seduction disguised as love. Humans are so desperate to love and be loved that, in the beginning, most are tricked into thinking this type of abuse is love especially if the abuse is happening on the psychic/spiritual levels.

Upon reading this section a friend told me, "When I was a reporter covering the courts, I remember an FBI agent suggesting that for kids who are abused, this is the most attention they've ever received. A loved child is less likely to invite this into their experience."

Love – An energy of the heart and soul. It expands and uplifts you when felt and expressed. It is the human emotion people most desire. When you feel love within, it spirals outward and connects you to all existence through the opening of the heart.

An example of psychic sexual abuse would be when a predator looks at a child or adult and establishes immediate deep contact. This contact can be made through a smile, wink, glance, look, conversation, or any opportunity to connect. On some level this connection is literally with the soul. They turn on the sexual energy (disguised as love) and move it into the sexual regions of the victim. Sexual arousal can happen at any age. Both the predator and the victim feel the energy, it excites them, and a secret bond is formed. The unsuspecting victim will remember this feeling until it is cleared. The energy can be ignited at any given moment by another predator fishing for a connection. Of course some predators are completely psychic at smelling this sort of energy. They can find it wherever it lays dormant ready to be awakened. This occurrence consistently happens under the radar, even with children who have the most astute guardians.

I am going to repeat several comments in this section. Why does both physical and psychic sexual abuse happen to children so often? It may seem easier to confront when it happens to an adult. People figure that an adult might be able to say no, or have some choice in the matter. Consequently most get very incensed when a perfectly innocent child is molested. **Were you molested as a child in some way?**

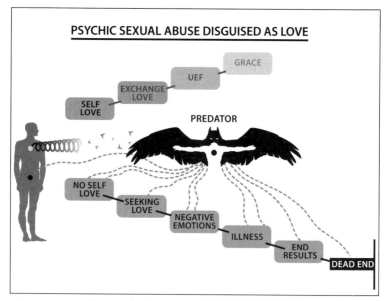

Diagram 10 - Psychic Sexual Abuse Disguised As Love

Do you have memories of this? Or do you have dreams about this, or feel this on some level but have no memory of anything happening? Not remembering an incident, but feeling like something happened, is a very common occurrence with many of the people I have worked with. Let's try to go deeper into your memories about these energies now.

SEXUAL HISTORY ⚹ EXERCISE 22

Take a look at your sexual history and answer these questions:

1. When was your first memory of sexual energy?

2. How old were you?

3. Who was connected to that memory?

4. Can you remember what happened?

5. How did it feel?

6. Did anything physical occur?

7. Was anything said, or expressed?

8. Was sexual energy disguised as love in any way?

9. How long did this situation persist?

10. Do you feel you were seduced?

11. Did you ever do this same thing to someone else? Even as a fantasy?

12. How do you feel about that?

13. Have these energies controlled you in any way?

14. Have these energies caused you to not trust the Power of Love?

SEXUAL HISTORY CONTINUED

15. Have these experiences tried to dominate your reality of life?

16. Do these energies make you sick?

17. Are you angry with these energies for controlling you?

18. Are you ticklish and extra sensitive around your pelvis and hips?

19. Has sexual abuse been in your family for many generations?

20. Are you ready to bring healing to your lineage?

21. Are you ready to experience the truth about love, healing, and exchange of Universal Energy Flow, which is free and clear of sexual abuse energy?

In The Reluctant Healer, *I told how living on the farm exposed me to Nature's reproductive forces at an early age. I also mentioned an experience with an older cousin that involved sexual energy when I was six. Fortunately, it was a minor incident, which left no real scars or damage; nevertheless, as I wrote before, I realized it would need to be cleared.*

The more deeply I delved into sexual abuse energy in my writing, the more this energy came to the surface, giving me the opportunity to practice my own healing. As I felt into this energy, I was able to intuit where it had entered my cousin's family and how it had then moved between family members once it was there (As you work with the Intuition section and this one you will learn how to do this for yourself).

In my case it was more along the lines of psychic sexual energy, because the physical contact was so minor. This made it even trickier for me to deal with. As I worked more deeply into my energy, I could feel where there was a tiny access point for this energy to be stimulated. I located it in my physical body, in my pelvis, and when I pushed into the area, it tickled. I knew from past experience this signified the location of foreign sexual energy.

Once I located it, I did a long breathing meditation (20 minutes) and got myself vibrating really high. Just as I could feel my essence entering my body, I asked it to help me clear this foreign invader. My essence showed me how the energy came in after my little brother died. Losing Jeffery was a pivotal moment for our family, and it created uncertainty for me about love. My mom went into shock, and she unconsciously withdrew her love. I felt this on a deep level as a 6 year-old child.

When the sexual energy came along—disguised as love from a trusted older cousin—it got in.

The more I breathed, the more I felt the old grief my family had suppressed emerge out of my body. There was a deep wail stored in my lower back that moved around to my pelvis, and when the emotions cleared my whole body started pulsing with energy even stronger. My essence moved all the way into my body. My pelvis vibrated so much that I started to feel heat in my base chakra/coccyx bone region and the abuse energy started moving up and out of my spine. My mind be-

came crystal clear. I realized it was cleansing the mental level, too, clearing the thought form that I could not trust love. This energy was wrapped around my spine and when it released, I completely relaxed. Finally my essence showed me the healing I was receiving on all levels, including the spiritual.

The biggest connection came to me when I was able to see how this energy had entered at a weak moment in my child-hood. I was looking for love and my body was holding grief, and this was exactly the situation these energies look for. I realized that my cousin was not aware of what he was doing. He was being controlled by whatever parasite existed within him, moreover he was only nine years old. That was also part of the spiritual healing because in the moment of realization, I was able to forgive him on the spiritual level. My essence showed me he was confused, looking for love, and acting out what had been done to him by others.

When all levels were clear I was able to weave the for-giveness and self-love back through the physical, emotional, mental, and spiritual bodies. As the healing continued, my essence showed me how this energy would try to sneak back in and cause me to believe I could not trust love. It would use the underlying memory from my brother's death and it would say to me, "You cannot trust love. It will abandon you when you are vulnerable. You better learn to take care of yourself."

When all of these pieces fell into place I was able to send love and gratitude to my cousin for helping me get this lesson. When I chose this final step – still in the breathing session – the exchange with the Universe went into overdrive; my heart opened completely. Suddenly I connected to the energy of the whale's heart, it was kind of bizarre to my mind, but my heart felt it, so I stayed with the connection. I could feel just how sensitive and loving the whale is, specifically the big Blue Whale. For some reason I intuitively knew so much about this gentle giant and its ability to love with its car-sized heart. Then I knew the Power of Love was limitless for me. All I had to do was choose love in any situation.

My essence connected me to my baby brother and his love for me flowed into my heart. His face came to me in that moment. I cried and spoke his name. He exchanged love to me for choosing to remember him. The Universal Energy Flow grew even stronger, and I thought my body was levitating. I started to laugh and joy filled me. Suddenly all of the grief I was carrying for my family was gone, everything came to a completion point. My body never felt better, my emotions never felt freer, my mind had never been so relaxed and open, and my spirit was content. It was a good day!

Special note to parents, guardians, and caretakers

I write this section not to scare or upset you, but to help you heal any of these energies in and around you, as well as alert you to instinctively recognize when such predator energies are present. The key to a healthy child is for you to love you in their presence. Be that example, so they can feel the beauty of exchange through love. If they are content with that realization, if the child is around an adult who loves him or herself and if the child in turn feels loved, they will not seek that connection outside and will not be lured in by a predator.

A child who feels loved and protected by a parent will in most cases let you know about the predator. You will see it in their behavior, and in many instances they will tell you if they do not want to be around that person. They may throw a fit and refuse to go near them. Of course discretion and intuition always bring more awareness to each moment. The key is to be aware. It is so much more empowering to make a conscious choice that protects your child, than having to hear about it and trying to resolve it years down the road. Remember to grow the love from inside you and your wings will extend over the ones you are protecting, giving their wings a chance to grow as well.

As I mentioned before, my situation was not so extreme, but what about children who were molested by an older person such as a family member, teacher, or stranger? Why does this happen so often? Why does this become the defining sexual moment for so many? Why does this early sexual abuse happen to those it happens to? Is it an accident? What draws the abuser to the victim, and the victim to the abuser? Why does sexual energy find its way to children so often? I will say this time and time again; they are open and looking for the feeling of love. Sexual predators carry the imprint of how to represent sexual energy as love. The innocents buy it hook, line and sinker.

Parenting is a 24/7, 365 day-a-year job. No matter how diligent parents are, if it is in the karma of the child, he or she will attract it in one brief moment with anyone, from a stranger to a family member. In order for the incident to be completely healed it has to be healed on all levels—physical, emotional, mental, and spiritual. When the sexual abuse energy is cleared, the disguised energy can no longer distort your experience around the Power of Love.

Let me make this point again: The sexual abuse most people carry may never have manifested into a physical molestation, and in many instances the physical experiences may be more easily confronted than the less tangible, psychic ones. The non-physical experiences get in on the energetic plane as deeply as the physical ones; they are disguised as love as well, therefore these experiences may land through a glance, gesture or smile in a split second. The energy lands into the physical body and it is felt as excitement, sexual arousal, sensuality, heat, and even vibration. The predator knows how to stimulate the sexual energy in a child in the same way one experiences it as an adult. This is what they seek. The purer the target, the more imprint they can leave in the child's energetic body, the better. Once these energies take hold in a victim they will run interference and create many short circuits in a person's energy, thoughts, and actions. Literally it can seem like something else is running the personality of the victim. This is where the Love of Power prevails, and predators love the feeling of being in total control of their victims—consciously or unconsciously.

Sexual abuse and sexual predator energies are very difficult for most people to spot, look at, and confront. Predator energies are masters at camouflage and deception. They have exceptional ability in gaining the trust of all parties involved, and can operate under the radar for years. Again, it is all presented under the umbrella of 'love.' An entity disguises itself so well most people think the negative energy is them. This is why these energies have so much power and create so many disturbances in people's lives.

Predators enlist the trust of everyone, even themselves. They believe their own stories about how trustworthy they are. The problem lies in the lies. The problem lies in the secrets they carry within their own abuse stories. They underestimate the strength, power, will, and seductiveness of the energy that resides within them. The negative thought form attaches to the DNA and passes down through the genes and lineage. It is that nefarious. It camouflages itself so well within the confines of the human psyche that most predators do not know they are host to an external entity. They do not know that this entity will live and feed off of their energy indefinitely, or that it has the ability to lie dormant throughout the life span if it so chooses. Nevertheless, not knowing these things does not excuse the predator from the responsibility associated with their actions. There is always awareness when the predator steps over the line with sexual energy, and there is no ignoring the feeling that something is wrong when the parasitic energy starts creating more destructive behavior.

Mistletoe is a master parasite in the plant kingdom. It can change shape to look like a pine needle, maple or elm leaf. It burrows into the branch of the host and sucks energy out of the tree. The tree believes the mistletoe is a part of it and willingly relinquishes its sap—its life force—so much so that oftentimes you see a dead tree with lots of round green balls of life on it. When that host is dead the mistletoe blooms and the seedpods burst open and fly to the next tree. It is a prolific parasite that you can see in wooded areas everywhere. The flowering mistletoes depend entirely on the host tree for nourishment. These scrubs are lethal parasites of conifers, such as pine, spruce, fir, and hemlock. The plant leaves and berries contain toxic chemicals that can be poisonous and the plant should be kept out of reach of young children who may be tempted to eat the berries.

In the photo you will have to look closely to see the mistletoe in the Blue Spruce tree. As long as the tree is alive the

mistletoe is hard to spot. There are close to fifty balls on the branches of this tree. Eventually the mistletoe will take the life of this tree if it is not strong enough to resist, and there will be a dead tree with green spheres of mistletoe remaining until it moves on to another host.

Once all of the life force is sucked out of the tree it will look like the next photo, a dead tree with fewer and fewer green balls because even the mistletoe has moved on now. Unfortunately you see a lot of these trees throughout the West. Between the drought, bark beetles and mistletoe, many evergreen trees are no longer ever-green.

Another fascinating characteristic of mistletoe is it tends to congregate in the tops of trees not unlike the negative

thought forms circulating in your head. The parasite knows where the freshest life force of the tree is most available—in the new growth at the top—likewise the parasitic energies that feed off of people like to attach to the energy of your thoughts and have free access to you. This is one of the most precise examples I can give you about these kinds of entities energies. They are very real and flourish in the bed of negativity. Most of the time people do not know that the energies/thoughts are not them.

Gus, a 44 year-old mechanic came to see me with a sense of urgency. He had been through surgery for testicular cancer and was getting ready for chemotherapy. He was very concerned the cancer would spread to other parts of his body. He said that cutting it out was one thing, but he was certain it was not the cause of the tumor. I agreed. I asked him had he ever been sexually abused. He could not remember anything, but he said there was quite a bit of sexual abuse in his family and that his mother and sister had both been raped. I told him I had several more questions like a diagnostic check of a car engine. He liked that and revealed he had problems with pornography and cocaine use, and he was on anti-depressants. When he lay on the table I checked his pelvic muscles and he was extremely ticklish to the touch. I explained to him that there were several indicators showing that he was carrying sexual abuse energy. He asked me to take it out. I told him it was not that easy and that he needed to increase his awareness with the energies so he could release them himself.

I showed him the breathing meditation, and he was very motivated to do the work. After breathing for 15 minutes his body started to vibrate very strongly. His emotions began to release and he opened his heart. I showed him how to work with his energy and how to move it through his body. Gus was quite ecstatic about what he learned and even more importantly he was able to identify one of the parasitic negative thought forms operating in him. It identified itself as a cold black energy that specialized in depression. This energy had convinced Gus on some level that it protected him and the real irony was the energy had moved into Gus when he was six, shortly after his mom had been raped.

When Gus felt free enough to speak to the energy he informed it that he no longer needed its protection and he released the energy to the light. I offered him specific guidance on how to clear this energy on the deepest levels and Gus did the work. That was our first session together and we continued on working until Gus cleared all the foreign energies out of his body. His experience with chemo and radiation treatment went very well, and his earlier fears about the cancer spreading have not played out.

When I speak of an entity it sounds like the Exorcist, right? It sounds like something very scary and demon-like. Yuck, who wants that? As I wrote in *The Reluctant Healer*, predator energies are very psychic, very calculating, very secretive, and very discreet. They know how to disguise themselves as love and operate through trust with you and your loved ones.

I am not trying to spook you here, but if there is sexual abuse in your family, then you have it somewhere in your DNA, too. Can this energy be illuminated and cleared out of the DNA, physical body, emotional body, mental body, and spiritual consciousness? I believe it can. However, it has to be dealt with on the spiritual plane. As above, so below. As below, so above!

As I said before, most people are trying to only address the abuse on physical, emotional, and mental levels and there's no doubt that this is also part of the healing process. However, trying to understand what happened psychologically does not completely heal the abuse because it does not clear all of the energy. In the worst cases it can make the energy stronger by twisting the psyche through confusion. Trying to heal the abuse through the emotions will often have the same effect because the sexual abuse energy will use the emotions as fuel to make itself even stronger. As the sexual abuse energy becomes activated, it can crescendo into an almost spiritual-like experience. It will enliven even the most depressed individual because they will feel what they think is love, refueling their hope that they have finally found what they are looking for.

Sexual abuse energy only has one route to its stronghold on a person and that is through the spirit. To heal such an event, or events, and the psychic scars from sexual abuse, requires firm commitment, desire, and faith. If you suspect you carry this energy somewhere in your consciousness, then it is time to shine the light on it.

Psychic sexual abuse energy creates confusion and all sorts of chaos that can literally thrust a person's essence out of their body when the psychic sexual abuse energy is strongest. It distorts a person's awareness, and can make one feel possessed and not responsible for his or her sexual behavior. It creates a short circuit in the energy field of a person and can cause them to be inconsistent and unstable. Even more powerful is the energy that penetrates the victim; this energy acts as a seed, and once it takes hold, it spreads to others (like mistletoe). In a matter of time, the victim often becomes the abuser. Because the energy leads its victims to believe it is love, it is easily perpetrated and propagated. Insidiously seductive, it creates other predators on the prowl. It is shocking how powerful it is, and it is disturbing how its destructive behavior manifests in the least likely of places.

Louie, age 55, came to me distraught about a call from his family in South America. His adult nephew had been accused of sexually molesting his own children, and the family thought Louie would have the most clarity on the issue. Louie had left his country and family at an early age because his father and older brothers had abused him. He figured it would be best for him to come to America and start over. He said his sisters were upset that he left, and apparently their elders had sexually abused most of the family. He said it had been going on for generations.

Louie was distraught because he had fondled his nephew when they were young. When his family called he thought they were going to accuse him. That did not happen, but he felt responsible for passing the sexual abuse energy on to his nephew. His family wanted him to come home and help them through the crisis. They were in turmoil because all of the skeletons were coming out of the closet. I shared as much information about this energy with Louie in as short a time as I could, and we worked a couple of times clearing the sexual abuse energy before he headed back to his family.

A few months later Louie reported that by the time he got to his country and met with his family the situation had cooled off. They had been counseled by the local priest and were instructed to go back to church, confess their sins, and move on. Louie was disappointed because nothing was resolved by his visit, he was told to not to bring it up. I suggested maybe it was a blessing and it would give him time to heal himself. He agreed and thought he would get more experience working with this energy before he returned to his family one day.

Sexual abuse energy can be viewed, as I referred to it earlier, as an entity. This energy has the ability to disguise itself as the person or part of their personality or a negative thought form. It is a parasite that feeds off the energy of the host.

Sexual abuse energy reveals itself in the body in many ways. Below are symptoms that keep showing up in people who are not aware of having been sexually abused or molested physically, but have psychic sexual abuse symptoms in just about every case.

PSYCHIC SEXUAL ABUSE ENERGY SYMPTOMS

- Attract sexual abuse as an adult
- Addiction to pornography
- Addiction to cocaine in conjunction with pornography
- Excessive sexual appetite
- Little, or no sexual appetite
- Pelvic area problems—second chakra—with ovary, testicle, prostate—reproductive organ issues—such as cancer, cysts, endometriosis, menstrual constipation, sciatica, impotency

- Negative imbalances acted out in destructive ways especially with extreme, aggressive, addictive behavior

- Consistent dreams about sexual abuse, and violence

- Extremely overweight

- Bulimia

- Sugar addiction

- Erratic emotional behavior

- Sexual promiscuity

- Predator tendencies—sexual attraction to young children

- Sexual fantasies that involve taking another's power away

- Attracting inappropriate sexual encounters with strangers

- Hips and pelvis turn inward

- Injuries to hips, pelvis, and tailbone

- Severe PMS

- Depression

- Constipation

These are just some of the symptoms I have seen reoccurring many times with people. You can find exceptions to each one if you need to. I am working with an overview to help you identify these energies in yourself and others. Many people do not know they are host to one of these parasitic energies until it is too late and the energy gets them into a negative situation. So, how do you spot these energies? You have to sense them intuitively; you have to smell them out. If you are really paying attention, you will not be so easily seduced into trusting carriers of these negative energies.

I gave an example of how I tracked this energy in my body from the aforementioned sexual incident with my cousin. As I wrote in The Reluctant Healer, *my older cousin and I were playing the farm version of the doctor game. My cousin wanted me to be the mother cow and he wanted to be the baby. He said he would try to suckle. I played along for a minute or two and when he put my penis in his mouth, it tickled and I peed. That ended the game. I remembered laughing and he got mad. I never really thought about it much in my life, but I have a photographic memory and very little eludes me. So, it was tucked away in there for me to deal with at a later time. I hope it is not too graphic for you, nevertheless we often learn the most through some of the more uncomfortable lessons.*

The point I want to make here is the ticklish feeling with my penis became a tracking symptom for me. Through that I was able to connect, and I think you can use this same symptom in your own search for these energies. The same feeling I felt when I was 6 years old, I felt several times in my life connected to my penis and pelvic area. A lot of the time around intimacy, and sexual moments not only would I feel ticklish, I would also slip back to a younger emotional time and state. That same emotional vulnerability I experienced when my brother died would come up. The thoughts about could I trust love, am I going to be abandoned or hurt? The trigger was the ticklish feeling.

I learned that the ticklish feeling was the energy that moved into me from my cousin in that brief moment and it was also the signifier that the energy was not mine. When I was ready to heal it, the energy exposed itself to me, showing me exactly where it was in my pelvis. As I described earlier, the breathing/energy work allowed me to access my spirit to complete the healing of the energy, which was held in place by the negative thought form, "You cannot trust love!"

As I mentioned before, I notice the psychic sexual abuse symptoms in these ways:

Attract sexual abuse as an adult *– It is never an accident when someone attracts sexual abuse. It is attracted or magnetized by the unconscious energy trapped in a person's body. Like attracts like.*

Addiction to pornography *– This huge business has some of the most psychically deviant energy in existence. It is built on the Love of Power. The creators of pornography know how to sow the seeds of sexual parasitic energy – like mistletoe! People who are addicted to pornography usually have problems with intimacy and use the sexual energy from pornography to stimulate themselves.*

Addiction to cocaine in conjunction with pornography *– This is the cocktail for those heavily under the influence of sexual abuse energy. In most cases there are vivid memories of molestation and the addition of cocaine is to recreate the high of the earlier experience. Sexual abuse energy has an extremely high charge of energy that feels like love to the victim.*

Sexual promiscuity *- excessive sexual appetite – The sexual abuse energy can push a person hard in their desperate search* *for love, and they hunger for connection through sex. These people shut down immediately after orgasm and become very cold. They have no interest in further intimacy.*

Little, or no sexual appetite *– When the person has shut down sexually on at least two levels (physical and emotional).*

Pelvic area problems (second chakra) *– The sexual abuse energy sows major distortions and conflict in the person's body. Oftentimes anger and sadness coalesce to create an acidic/toxic condition in the body.*

Negative imbalances acted out in destructive ways especially with extreme, aggressive, addictive behavior *– Discussed in the earlier sections in detail.*

Have consistent dreams about sexual abuse, and violence *– This is where a person's unconscious brings up the energy for it to be worked with, understood, and cleared.*

Extremely overweight *– The sexual abuse energy has created an extreme state of vulnerability and weight is used to try and provide a buffer or protection.*

Bulimia *– I understand it affects a small percentage of males; however, my experience is working with girls and women on this issue. The sexual abuse energy gets in and creates distortions around the emotions of girls just prior to puberty. Usually bulimia is a reaction that kicks into high gear as the hormones increase and sexual attention starts to come in from the outside. This energy works to convince young girls that they are not loveable the way they are, that they are not skinny enough, and not attractive enough.*

Sugar addiction – *Sugar is used as a sedative to decrease the discomfort around the emotions, which are pulled on and twisted by the sexual abuse energy.*

Erratic emotional behavior – *Multifaceted condition can be made more extreme by sexual abuse energy, oftentimes connected to many other symptoms such as bulimia, sugar addiction, overweight, sexual promiscuity, etc.*

Predator tendencies – *Sexual attraction to young children. These symptoms are very secretive and hard to spot, you have to use your intuition to track these energies in the least likely places.*

Sexual fantasies that involve taking another's power away – *These are situations you are not usually aware of until you get to know a person intimately, or you get involved with people who actively play out these roles. The pornography industry uses this as a major market because so many people have these scenarios active in their life experience.*

Attracting inappropriate sexual encounters with strangers – *Sexual abuse energy causes a person to take risks for excitement, and spurs them to seek love from the outside.*

Hips and pelvis turn inward – *Sexual abuse energy begins to manifest in physiological ways in the body, and it is easier to spot than some because you can see it in the appearance of the body.*

Injuries to hips, pelvis, and tailbone – *These situations become self-evident when they happen time and time again with some people. They are not an accident.*

Severe PMS – *The most extreme cases tend to show up as sexual abuse energy.*

Depression – *Sexual abuse energy can suck the life force out of a person like mistletoe on a tree.*

Constipation – *Sexual abuse energy can create emotional blockages in the second chakra, which will create a physical block in the colon.*

SUMMARY OF SEXUAL ABUSE ENERGY

In this section I have spoken in depth about sexual abuse energy. This energy has a Love of Power. It disguises itself as love and tries to control people by getting them to doubt the true Power of Love. It reinforces the illusion that love hurts and cannot be trusted. It is a parasitic energy that takes energy from you and feeds off of your life force. This energy has the ability to create its own intelligence system within your own psyche blocking access to Universal Energy Flow. As an entity, it has the ability to cause most of the negative afflictions affecting mankind. That's a big statement, but this is what I have found to be true.

If sexual abuse energy at its core has the ability to influence humans to not love, and to not trust love, then it wins. It is then able to persuade us to seek out all external ways to feel good. So, if you can follow my reasoning, you can see this is a very powerful force. You could call this energy the devil, Satan, or by any other negative name. It is a powerful force I will admit, and at its center there is the greed exerted as a Love of Power, a will to dominate others.

Sexual abuse energy can only be completely healed one way—spiritually. Abuse energy has to be brought out into the light, it has to be exposed and disentangled from the person. It has to be brought forth in a way that a person can safely experience the lie that was imprinted around love in the moment the abuse energy first entered the person. Memories do not have to be recalled, rather the lie has to be exposed in a controlled safe environment. It also has to happen in a conscious state, not under hypnosis, or induced by drugs. It takes total clarity. All the levels—physical, emotional, mental, and spiritual—have to be brought together consciously. The healing that has been missing is the weaving of it all together in the spiritual realm through the Power of Love. As I wrote earlier the Power of Love is the key. Here is a reminder from Section 1:

> Love connects you to you. From that vantage point you are then connected to everything, everywhere. Love is… Without this connection to love you will be lost, continually looking outside of yourself for love to fix you. At times you may think you have found it. However, when it is based in someone or something outside of you it will always fail to complete the spiral of love, because it is a straight line between whatever is outside and you. Love from inside you emanates from a circular center point, from the center of your heart chakra…The energy of love moves in and out of the heart chakra in a spiral. When you connect to your heart, to the love inside of you, you will always remember the Power of Love.

Your Right To Be

Take your power back, now!

Love.

Love yourself, trust and invest in the Power of Love.

Let the Universal Energy Flow through you as you open your heart to love. The choice to love is yours.

The choice to love you, is yours.

Love.

Love now.

Be free!

Many people are waiting for this healing. I have visualized a clinic that specializes in the healing of this condition. It will need lots of support to become a reality, and continued support to work effectively with those who are carrying these energies. Ultimately sexual abuse is a cry for love. Let's heal this problem by treating it at the core with love.

Mike, a 42 year-old man, came to see me for healing work. We worked on the sexual abuse energy that he said he carried from his father. He had distinct memories of his father fondling him as a young boy from age 6 to 11. He healed much awareness around how this energy caused him to not only mistrust, but also to be angry at love. Mike was mad, and felt like he had been manipulated into this life by the Universe. I told him it was time to forgive, and we worked out a plan for him to bring forgiveness into his life and an eventual healing with his father. He started to work on this by:

1. *Doing the breath work every day – he worked with the Sexual Healing CD in particular, talked about in Section 4.*

2. *To release his pent-up anger and hostility at the Universe, he practiced self-love and exchange daily (Review Section 1).*

3. *He had a job where he was able to bring awareness to others for healing. He felt like he was a healer because people always asked him for advice.*

4.   *We scheduled a healing with his father.*

This is where it got really interesting for Mike. Everyone around him noticed how much he was changing, how open he had become. But two days before he was to bring his father in for a healing session, which his father had agreed to, he was picked up for being in the wrong place at the wrong time. Apparently he stopped at a cruising location and had approached an undercover officer. Needless to say this influenced the process and brought the work to an end for that time. His father had to bail him out of jail, and he was too ashamed to meet with him after that. The important point here is the way these unresolved energies work; they will take down the ship just as things are about to be healed. I have watched this in negative, addictive, sexual abuse energies for years. Not only did the energy stop the healing process, but Mike also dropped out of his life and dropped many other relationships for quite some time.

Eventually Mike reappeared and said he was ready to pick up where he left off and begin the work again. I said we would need to start over. He agreed, and we are having more success this time around. Although he is still waiting to do the clearing with his dad, he has been able to do the healing on more levels, especially with his anger. He has to let go of the last bit of anger towards his father, which is keeping him stuck in the past and not moving forward to allow self-love or Universal Energy Flow to heal his spirit. One day Mike called to say his father was dying of cirrhosis of the liver from years of drinking. He feels like he has little time left to meet with his dad. I have assured him that the healing can take place inside him with or without his dad's confession.

The focus has been on clearing the sexual energy inside of him. Time will tell if he will cleanse it through the spirit. I always look at healing from the spiritual level. That's why I say that while the physical, emotional, and mental are important, it is imperative to address the most important aspects with the spirit so that the healing is complete.

The work is ongoing with Mike. These situations are incredibly instructive for me as I see how hard it is for the victim to forgive the abuser. Mike now knows he has to release his father to heal. I will be interested to see how all of this plays out.

Debbie, a 38 year-old, nurse has been seeing me for years. We have been working on healing a rape incident off and on during this time. Just as she would close in on cleaning up the final pieces she would fall off the bandwagon. Some of this was due to a lack of discipline with self-love and exchange with Universal Energy Flow; as a result she would go and binge on sugar, generally an entire cheap white cake from the supermarket. I have watched this fluctuation yo-yo her weight up and down 30-50 pounds in a matter of months. I feel her get so close, and then one small disturbance and she goes sideways. Stopping when healing is so close is a very common occurrence with sexual abuse energy. The entities will fight to stay in control of a person and use any means they can to do so.

Debbie's situation stemmed from being the hot young sexy blonde in her twenties. She loved her ability to get attention. One night, when she had been drinking heavily, she was raped in the parking garage outside her apartment. She had some very vivid descriptions of this young black man as being handsome. The attacker was never caught, but it was almost as if she did not want him to be caught. Of course I met her many years after the event, and she had done lots of work on it with her therapist. What was interesting was she had started dating black men after this though she could never attain the level of excitement she felt the night of the rape. She carried scars from that night, but it was complex because it also excited her. This is one of the perverse ways these energies work!

Deep down I know she does not want to experience this complexity, and in our work she realized that she had been carrying a lot of sexual energy her entire life. We tracked it into early childhood and found some situations where she re-membered having sexual dreams and fantasies when she was as young as age 6 and 7. We even tracked the energy in her psychically and found the energy flowed into her from her mom, who had an affair while she was pregnant with her. She had a few memories of her mom meeting with a man who al-ways bought her things when she was young. Just as we would be working to connect all of the dots, she would fall out and disappear. I have learned not to take any of this personally.

She is still in and out with her process, nevertheless, she knows on some deep level she has to heal this in her life, and she trusts this work so much she sends all of her loved ones with similar issues to see me. Deep down I know she will heal this eventually, in her own time. I know this because she is so intent on helping others, she says she feels a responsibility to help others even if she cannot help herself. The Universe has a plan for people, so I remain patient with her. As she heals I know she will be an even better role model for those suffering from similar scars.

A few other interesting points we have uncovered with Debbie have been her physical situation with her weight. After she was raped she fell into a depression, and was put on medication. About eight months afterwards she began to gain weight. Her doctor said the problem was her thyroid and put her on more medication. So, in addition to anti-depressants, she began taking thyroid medication. It seems many sensitive women start to gain weight about eight months after starting anti-depressants, and then are diagnosed at the same time with a slow thyroid.

I have seen it enough to know it is an issue, and I wonder why it is not being written about, especially with the suggestion that anti-depressants are slowing the thyroid down, compounding the problem in the physical body. Likewise Debbie became more anxious about the weight and she was soon taking anti-anxiety as well as sleep medication. The point of this is, if the healing does not occur at the causation point, it is likely to be a long road of wild goose chases for the symptoms, a road that does not bring the healing that people deserve.

CANCER

I have worked with quite a number of cancer patients. It is always uncomfortable work for me because I feel the pressure these people are under. Cancer is an intense wakeup call. I know it is not about me, but I do like to help people to the best of my ability and I know cancer plays for keeps. I have noticed the people who seem to do the best have the most positive attitudes, and have decided to use cancer as the sign to change their life. I support them in this awakening. The ones who I notice having more difficulty are the ones who change very little.

In *The Reluctant Healer* I stated that I believed cancer was a response to anger being held in the body, and I had more than one cancer patient react harshly to this comment. In each case I gently observed the reaction and realized it was due to the unresolved anger being pushed to the surface. I will never assert that I am an expert with this disease. Generally people come to me after they have elected to do the Western medicine approach to cancer treatment. I work with them and whatever their decision about treatment. I feel like it is my job to help them get clear of the cause of the cancer, and to let Western medicine do what it does. It is the healing that's important and I assist any way I can.

> *I have recently heard from a good friend who has cancer and has just started chemotherapy. Her oncologist told her she had to relax, let go of stress, and give up her anger for the treatment to work. When I heard this I smiled and said she's exactly right! I applaud the allopathic doctors who understand the whole picture with their patients and address them on all the levels. There needs to be more integration between science and spirit when it comes to health and well-being.*

I find cancer festers and grows in an acidic place of chronic negativity within a person. This stems from the same 'lack of love' place as all of the aforementioned negative scenarios. Why not choose love to heal oneself now and forever? Surely you do not need to get sick to wake up? With a cancer patient I up the ante, because I know with some of them they are on limited time. I help them get to the core of the negative belief about love. We start at this point and work to clear unresolved anger around the specific area where the cancer has metastasized in the body. We do our best to uncover what they are angry about, and the thought forms associated with this anger. All anger stems from a place of not feeling loved or loveable. The Power of Love is the true healer, and if we can shift the awareness around this with cancer patients, their condition changes right along with it.

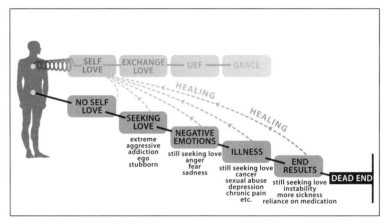

Diagram 11 - No Self-Love - no support for the process of healing

CANCER ~ EXERCISE 23

Do you have cancer?
Have you had cancer in your life?
Do you worry about getting cancer?
If cancer is in your space (physically, mentally, or genetically), take the time to love yourself as deeply as possible.

1. Give the information in this book a try.
2. Commit to the discipline of daily breath work.
3. Let go of all upset.
4. Answer the wakeup call. What do you have to change in your life?
5. Do it now.

Choose love and life, and exchange with the Universe. If you love enough you can heal anything!

MARRIAGE AND DIVORCE

What is going on with couples today? Marriages that end in divorce happen with astonishing frequency for modern-day partnerships, however the only event that people celebrate and truly acknowledge is the marriage. Marriage is society's container for normalcy, it holds our dreams of what it is to complete the human experience: to fall in love, get married, have children, and live happily ever after! Most couples do not want to hear the statistics about how many marriages do not survive when planning the big day. Certainly our families prefer not to hear such forecasts either. Everyone wants to believe in the dream, so I will not spoil it with statistics. Is it the modern era that is responsible for so much divorce? Is it simply that people are no longer willing to live an illusion if things are not working? Do people complete their karma together faster in these times?

Would we be willing to acknowledge that two people were ill-fated when they tied the knot, but they experienced three good years together? Perhaps as a result of the relationship a beautiful child came into the world. Maybe these two were actually 'oil and water' and were not meant to blend together for the long haul. Nevertheless, the child may have been the reason they came together and, unbeknownst to them, the soul of this particular child may have actually brought them together. Think about it. I know it is time we look beyond measuring the success of a marriage by how many years people stay together. Do not get me wrong, I am not advocating divorce, I am advocating a new approach to this reality.

How many times have you leaped before you looked? Do we then pass the verdict that the couple should never have even attempted to live the dream? Or could we conclude, "Great experience, something learned. Learning what I do not want, has shown me what I do want." Look at all you learned in those three short years, look at how much you realized about how flexible you could be. Look at this beautiful child! Notice the wonderful ingredients this child has in his or her DNA, the wonderful mixture of oil and water.

Would it be a glorious day when two people choose to celebrate the time they did spend together?

MARRIAGE AND DIVORCE
EXERCISE 24

1. Have you been through a divorce, or a painful breakup?

2. What scars has it left you to heal before you open yourself to a new relationship?

3. Is some part of you waiting to be healed spiritually before you blindly leap into another's arms with the hope they are going to be the 'one?'

4. Do you have to love you first?

Divorce is too often associated with long drawn-out court battles and custody hearings. In my experience the couples who are arguing and fighting over every last piece of furniture or dollar are not ready to let go of the relationship. The drama can be addictive. What if the pattern of blame and anger could be broken? What if there was a spiritual releasing process that carries as much weight as marriage to bring about the circle of completion? As sensitive sentient beings I believe we could benefit by honoring and celebrating divorce in an equal energetic ceremonial setting to marriage.

Rather than trying to fight it out in court, why not bring the witnesses back together for a releasing ceremony? All could honor the time together, even if it was conflicted, without the need for blame or finding fault. The ritual can allow the couple to own up to their incompatibility and acknowledge their effort, designate the time together as sacred, or at the least as being real, instead of trying to nullify, deny or bury it in regret. Acknowledge the witnesses of the marriage for holding space, and allow them to release their investment in the relationship. Celebrate the process, divide the belongings, and make agreements about how to move forward in life.

If children are involved, the couple can state their intention about remaining peaceful. Make a commitment about how to parent this child or children in a healthy modern-day lifestyle. Vow to support them, regardless of what their parents choose to do in or out of marriage.

Are we as a culture ready to drop the negative stigma that divorce equals failure? Not yet it seems. Guilt is a powerful tool that many people choose to live with and assess their actions by, especially when it comes to divorce. But think about it, what if we honored the experience together as a success, and worked to complete it in an up-lifting way? We need to establish a new way of celebrating time spent together even if it is a different span of time than our parents' or grandparents' marriages. Just as with our food and computers, today's relationships happen much faster. It is time to create new rituals that address the realities of our relationships today.

The relationship I was using in the example above was my own marriage. I choose to see it as a positive experience, and I do my best to view it on that level. I know it has been a positive experience for my daughter when I have kept things positive with her mother. Any time I look back and find regret creeping into the picture, I catch myself and move forward to all I have to be grateful for. I have a beautiful daughter. She is happy and I am happy that she is happy and she feels love inside herself for herself. Mission accomplished! I still have work to do being her father, friend, and ally the rest of our days together, though I am able to sleep well at night knowing she loves herself. She has a wonderful awareness of the many choices she has as to how to live her life. Her mom and I get along very nicely these days. If we were not getting along I would suggest a healing ceremony for our divorce. In this case it does not appear we need it.

The choice to love you is your choice, not someone else's. The choice to exchange this love with the Universe is yours. If this kind of healing is something you are interested in, let me know, I am willing to lead these ceremonies. I intend to write more about this topic, and these ceremonies are applicable to any committed relationship. I am willing to do my

MARRIAGE AND DIVORCE
EXERCISE 25

1. Has divorce, or a nasty breakup created a place where energy feels stuck inside of you, your family, children or pets that is waiting to be healed?

2. Is it time for a healing? Or are you waiting for your ex to be the one who initiates the healing, or say they are sorry?

3. How long do you intend to wait?

4. Does the power to forgive and move on reside in someone else, or inside of you?

part to bring more peace to the planet. It is time to bring an end to this conflict, and what better way than to take a look at intimate relationships.

INTIMATE RELATIONSHIPS

Someone asked me recently, "Why are you not in an intimate relationship? Isn't that a signal that something is wrong?" I said, "Well, it could be, I won't profess to have it all figured out. However, the place where you and I are different is: I do not place a prize on being in a relationship with someone else. My primary work right now is the balance, understanding and completeness of relationship within myself. This focus is bearing fruit in the writing of this book, and is the corner-stone to all the healing work I teach and do.

"I do not feel any lack of relationship, maybe to a fault. I am not saying this would work for everyone, but it has for me. It is the work I have been doing with myself for the last several years. It has not gotten boring and, if you can wrap your mind around this, I feel like I am already in relation-ship with my next partner and it's going great! Just because she has not materialized into physical form creates no basis for success, or failure in my way of thinking. I am learning to be patient in this life. I know her voice, her touch, and her scent. I know her through my feminine side. We have jour-neyed together many times; I am in no rush to be in tandem right now. The time does come for all things."

My friend looked at me and said, "I never thought of it that way." I smiled and said, "I know. That's why I explained it to you." He could not quite let it go and asked, "But don't you get lonely?" Patiently, I replied, "Sometimes, I'm human.

*But most of the time I am perfectly content. I am in relation-
ship with myself and with the Universe. There does not need
to be a person in physical form." He said, "How can you feel
like you know her already? Do you know her? Is she someone
you know?" I realized he was reluctant to trust the message,
but I patiently persevered replying, "I do not think I have
physically met her in this lifetime. But I have known her
in so many lifetimes. She has been my lover, my mother, my
daughter, my sister, my brother, my father, my son—she has
been in a multitude of relationships to me. I know her, and
she knows me. She is I, I am she. She is within me, and I am
within her."*

*My friend laughed and said, "I guess it would be too much
to expect this first relationship I am in to be that deep. We
can't seem to get past who hurt whose feelings and, 'Are you
going to leave me or not?' I don't think it would do either of
us any good to try and think about knowing each other from
another time." This time I smiled and said, "Have patience
my friend, Rome was not built in a day."*

*Sara, a 38 year-old schoolteacher, claimed she was destined to
be an old maid. I kept telling her if she would do the internal work all of her dreams would come true. Even with her
doubts she was a good student and followed these steps:*

1. *She took on the personal discipline to work with herself. She said she did the breathing meditation every
   day for a year and showed me her calendar. She was
   consistent. Better than me!*
2. *She refined her connection to her energy, and learned
   how to generate love inside of herself through the discipline of breathing.*

INTIMATE RELATIONSHIPS: IMAGINATION ⸱ EXERCISE 26

1. Imagine your perfect partner. What does he or she look like? How do they walk, talk, smile, play, etc.? What do you feel like as you envision the two of you together? Give yourself permission to go all out with this exercise. Dream it! Spend as much time on it as you desire. Is this partner the one you have been waiting for?

2. Look inside yourself now and see if you can imagine this person. Allow them to be real. This is not a fantasy. If you can imagine it, the process has begun, and it is real because it has happened inside of you.

3. Your partner is you. Accept it, make peace with it, and let yourself be filled with love. Let the birds sing around you. Let the Universal Energy Flow through you, to you, and back out. Grace accumulates and as the Universal Energy Flows out of you in a complete circle of expression, guess what happens? You manifest the love you are seeking internally and externally. Completion!

3. *Through her love and connection to the Universe, she became much more positive, and confident about herself.*

4. *She connected the dots about just how powerful she was when she was clear.*

5. *She started to help other teachers let go of stress by introducing them to the breathing.*

6. *She started manifesting new friends, and just at this time, a wonderful man came into her life.*

7. *Her partner was a man, not one of the 'wounded boys' from her past; she had created a partner who she immediately felt seen by and safe with.*

8. ***She got it. The Universe recognized what to send her because she had clearly communicated it outward from inside her.***

9. *She completed the circle.*

10. *A balanced healthy man, who understood her, and with a sense of humor! He was interested in her spiritual journey, she did not have to change, or give anything up. He wanted it all! Sara is doing so much good in the world and helping so many. I wish there were more people like her who were willing to do the work. As I mentioned earlier, patience is a virtue!*

LEADERSHIP ROLES

One of the more challenging roles as a leader is how to navigate relationships when you are the one in charge. You will play many roles for people in your leadership position whether it is parent, teacher, boss, etc. It comes with the territory. It is not all glamorous. Many projections will come your way; they will not necessarily depend on age, sex, sexual preference, looks, charm, or any other characteristic. They may depend more on the type of leading you do, and the type of people you have around. As an authority figure, you may as well accept the responsibilities that come with the job. How you deal with the responsibilities will ultimately determine how much fun you will have. When I play the leader role I have found it pays to have a whole lot of patience and humor.

LEADERSHIP ROLES
EXERCISE 27

1. Which position do you feel you occupy the most—leader or follower?

2. How do you fare in either? Are you needy, difficult or rebellious as a follower? Are you stiff, controlling, and domineering as a leader?

3. Are you able to maintain clear boundaries with people and not be a tyrant?

4. How do you lead, and play the various roles required of you to be an effective teacher and connect with others in a meaningful way?

5. How do you allow the Universe to be teaching you at the same time you are working with the people who are coming to you?

From personal experience I can say being a spiritual teacher has many colors and flavors. I love helping people wake up. I love helping people who take full responsibility for their behavior and students who are conscious and mindful with all of their projections and reactions. Not everyone who comes to me will have this level of self-awareness and I accept playing many roles for people. Of course discretion/ discernment is not just for leading spiritual work. Consider police officers, security guards, therapists, bank tellers, and gatekeepers of any kind. If you have authority you will probably feel the wrath of people's judgment and dissatisfaction at different times, especially if you exhibit a Love of Power and abuse this leadership role.

From a Universal perspective we are always in the classroom, no matter what seat we are sitting in. Having the consciousness and awareness that you expect others to have is a necessity as a leader. Nevertheless, retaining the perspective that you are a fallible human being and that you are a work in progress is necessary in order for you to be able to relax and enjoy the ride. 'Be yourself' is good advice, but sometimes easier said than done.

I try to look at it all as a circle. I have been the rebellious, reluctant student many times. It is unreasonable for me to expect that people will never be difficult or resistant. Karma is a circle. What I have done I also have to deal with and have compassion for—to a degree. I like to say it takes one to know one. Sometimes we need to be witnessed for exactly who we are, and be acknowledged for our hurt, resistance, stubbornness, and lack of trust. It does not matter whether you are a leader or a follower, if you want to change your experience of life, you will have to give up your obsessive interests in past hurts, and the old patterns and expectations that come with them.

If you are a leader you are a follower. If you are a follower you are a leader. It is a circle. What goes around comes around. What you resist persists. Maybe a person who calls him or herself a leader is willing to get the metaphor of it all a little faster than someone who resists his or her own leadership qualities. I relate to this quote by Yogi Bhajan:

> *If you want to learn something, read about it. If you want to understand something, write about it. If you want to master something, teach it.*

It all depends on the experience you are looking for.

This section is in the book because I know many of you are leaders. I train people to be healers, and I train healers to be leaders. What additional responsibility comes with your job? Who really is your employer? I want you to think beyond the job and occupation to the bigger picture. As you get the bigger picture you will have more access to Universal Energy Flow, which will result in love, exchange, and creativity. I guarantee that if you do this you will never worry about job security. You will be having a great time at the activity you call 'work'. Who knows, you may even start to think of your 'work' as 'play'. You may grow to marvel at the way the Universe is leading you through this thing called life, work, and career.

Role as a follower
EXERCISE 28

- How do you show up in your role as a follower?

- Do you project lots of energy (love, needs, judgments) towards the leader?

- Do you rebel?

- Do you expect a leader to carry your pain?

- Are you the teacher's pet?

- Do you expect the leader to take on your drama because of the way you are exchanging with them?

- Do you always work to get close to the leader in some way?

- Are you the leader's pain in the behind?

- Are you needy with this person?

- Do you respect their private time?

- Do you work to prove yourself invaluable to them?

EXERCISE 28 CONTINUED

- Do you feel more comfortable if you can create their reliance on you?

- Do you work to create an intimate flow of energy from them?

- Do you use your relationship with the leader to work out your issues regarding your worth and self-esteem? Are you hungry for the leader's love and approval?

- Do you compete for their attention?

- Do you set up romantic scenarios in your mind?

- Do you try to seduce the leader?

- Do you create karma with these people?

- Do you create ways to pull on the leader's energy at times when they are most vulnerable?

- Do you look to find fault with the leader, so you can have your way out when things get tough?

ROLE AS A LEADER ⚞ EXERCISE 29

- How do you show up as a leader?

- Do you project lots of energy towards people who look to you for leadership?

- What are your expectations from students?

- Do you exhibit a lack of patience towards them when they are needy?

- Do you get sloppy with your boundaries?

- Do you allow yourself to develop romantic feelings and/or situations with your students?

- Are you clear about the roles you play with your students?

- Do you seek out favorites?

- Do you allow certain students to overstep boundaries with you because they are 'special?'

- Do you allow yourself to become put off by certain people because of some quality, trait, or behavior?

- Are you confident in your role as the leader?

- Are you confident in your role as an authority figure?

MONEY

My idea of money totally fits under the definition of exchange. When people come to me complaining about money issues I ask:

+ Where are you stuck?

+ Where is your energy stuck?

+ Where are you feeling under-appreciated?

+ Where are you pissed off?

+ What's the exchange?

+ Who are you holding hostage or blaming for your lack?

+ Are you punishing your family with your anger by underachieving, and struggling?

+ When are you going to allow yourself to be successful?

+ When are you going to get exchange balanced and flowing?

+ When are you going to love yourself?

Money - Any medium of exchange that is widely accepted in payment for goods and services and in settlement of debts. Money also serves as a standard of value, worth, or flow of resources.

Exchange – The flow of consciousness given and received as energy, respect, value, appreciation, and love. It can also refer to goods, services and money.

If you have been working with this book this will all be clear to you. If you are rebelling and you are stuck, then you may feel like this does not make sense and get pissed off. If you are angry then you get to remain in blame mode and you do not have to be present or accountable for your situation. If this is the case, it tells me you prefer to be stuck in your past. Did you think this section was going to be about the economy? I am joking here, but I also am very serious. I will say it again: Are you holding your family hostage (through blame or guilt) for your struggle with money, or success? How boring has that become?

Turn your life around now. In the last question I could replace family with government, IRS, business partner, lover, mortgage company, etc. If you are stuck in any of these places, then your exchange is off. The flow of consciousness given and received as energy, respect, value, appreciation and love is off; forget about goods, services, and money. It is about the spiritual side of the equation, and it always is! Fix the spiritual side around exchange and money will start flowing. As much as you think the fix is going to come from outside resources, I'm telling you this issue is inside of you. If you want to be wealthy with a sustainable flow of resources, learn to love you and exchange with the Universe. If you are able to have a spiritual connection to what you do to earn income, then your work becomes something that lifts you up. It exchanges back to you.

How much money do you need? Debt and reckless spending of money to try and feed the negative human traits will only create more dead ends and frustration. Who wants that?

No amount of money will give you self-love. Some of the unhappiest people I have met have also been some of the wealthiest. If you can love you and exchange love with the Universe and allow your creativity to flow, you will attain success. When that happens, it is good to let the Universe show you what to do with its money. We all have a spiritual life purpose that connects us to the Universe. It is a circle. The more exchange that is happening with the Universal Energy Flow, the more success you will acquire to exchange with and to keep in circulation with the Universe. Do the work to open yourself to the magic of the Universe and money will flow on the wings of love and exchange!

MONEY - EXERCISE 30

1. Write about your relationship with money. Take as long as you need.

2. Write about any similarities with your views on money and those of your family.

3. Do you feel like there is not enough money?

4. Do you feel abundant no matter how much money you have?

5. Does money own you?

6. Are you willing to trust money to flow to, around, and through you?

7. Are you open to money?

Most people have issues with money no matter how much they have or do not have. The more I play with the idea of exchange and the Universe being my employer, the more freedom I experience with the flow of money in my life. Give it a try.

Money has been something I have studied, worked on and opened up to in my life. Many people have commented on the line in The Reluctant Healer, *"I am open to money flowing 360 degrees around and through me, no matter what the source, as long as it is positive" (82). I butted heads with my father growing up about money and the control exerted with it. I felt like he was too frugal. He consistently emphasized that money and material objects would not make me happy. He would say, "Do you own things or do they own you?"*

It made a mark on me. It seemed I attracted a number of friends in my life who were determined to buy happiness and self-esteem through purchasing things such as clothes and luxury items. I would observe their spending patterns, and I would watch their debt grow. Many of these friends accused me of saving my money too much. I have always left those comments alone and realized the balance with money and material objects is inside of me. If I am loving myself and exchanging with the Universe, then I can clearly see that my five-year old Subaru is a gorgeous car. I was guided to trade in my gas guzzling V-8 SUV several years ago for the economically friendly Subaru. I do not let things own me, probably to a fault. I respect my things, I do not mind spending money and most of the time I feel incredibly abundant. Occasionally, if I watch enough news I may start to wonder about the dollar and our economy; however, when I turn the television off, within minutes I feel abundant again. I cannot control the external world regarding money, what I can control is my experience in it and my experience is a good one!

I am incredibly grateful for my father and the lessons he taught me about money, abundance, saving, investing, growing, and spending. I grew to appreciate the wisdom in my father's teachings. I feel very clean with money in every relationship in my life. To the best of my knowledge I do not owe anybody any money, and it is a good feeling to have. This feeling is helping me write this book, it is helping me study more deeply into love, exchange, and Universal Energy Flow. I am free in my relationship with money, because it does not own me.

Stewart, a 36 year-old entrepreneur came to see me frustrated about feeling stuck. I asked him about exchange in his life, and his answers seemed to be hiding something about money. Something was off in the picture and I kept probing. I looked directly into his anger and found the culprit. It was $80,000 of credit card debt. It started in college. He was angry at his family for not helping him more. He charged his way through life and used credit to try and ease his feelings of not being supported by his family or the Universe. Interestingly enough he had been through all of the 'New Age' courses about the secrets of money and wealth, and he knew all the terminology. But he could not lower his credit card debt for some reason. Unknown to him this debt was very important to his personality, I brought all of this to his attention, telling him his flow of money and exchange with the Universe was stuck because he was stuck. Specifically, his energy was stuck in the emotion of anger at not feeling supported by his *family in his early 20s. He got mad at me and refused to see the connection. I encouraged him to set them free and find the ways they had helped him learn about support. I asked him to embrace the opposite of what he thought was the problem. The more he worked into the dynamic with his family, the more freedom he began to experience in his flow of money and resources. As he paid down his credit card debt amazingly his life started to function in very open ways across the board. An intimate relationship that he had also been waiting for showed up, his business became much more successful, and best of all he became lighter and more happy. His connection to the Universe and the feelings of support blossomed.*

section four

THE HEALING WORK

The Healing Work

A re you ready to lighten up? Because guess what… the heavy lifting is done! The rest of the book will be lighter and easier to engage with. It's time to sit back and enjoy the ride as I cover a brief history and examples of the healing tools I use in the work. Enjoy these last sections, and don't hesitate to go back and review any areas that are still pulling on your attention.

HEALING TOOLS

In this section I will give an overview of the tools I use most frequently in the healing work. If you want a more complete description, refer to *The Reluctant Healer*, where I give more details on the healing session, breath, and other tools that I use. That said, I will hit on the main points here so you have the resources to understand this work.

I talk about energy, clairaudience, intuition, spirit, breath work, essential oil blends, Meditation CD's, and Universal Energy. These are what I would consider the primary tools in the work and they can help you become a healer.

The last statement may have jarred you a bit. I am sure many of you are reluctant to consider yourself a healer, but you are reading here so let us assume you are open to learning more about healing or using this information to heal something within yourself. If that's the case, I am fine. Let's do that! You will be a healer for yourself. Great!

At some point, if you become less stuck and cultivate personal healing, then you may share your experience or hand this book to a friend. At that point you may actually be helping another person heal. Even so, we do not have to call you a healer of others. I understand where that reluctance comes from and I am fine with it.

HOW THE BREATH WORK FOUND ME

I have to admit that before I experienced my first breathing session, I felt like I was about to explode in my life. Things were coming to a head; my spirit was pushing me to open up. I was stuck! My intuitive gifts were combusting and I had to learn how to use them positively to heal myself, otherwise they were making certain experiences much more difficult, in particular the relationship with my girlfriend.

Have you had difficulty with relationships lately? My gift of clairaudience, or intuitive hearing, was making it impossible for me to be with the person I was trying to be intimate with. I could hear her thoughts and I would experience her dreams. I could hear the truth when she spoke it and the lies every time she lied. I knew things were not working. I asked God to send me some answers. About this time strangers started grabbing me and telling me I was a healer; strangers on airplanes, on the street, in stores. I thought they were nuts, but it kept happening. Finally, when the relationship ended, my heart aching, my ears ringing and popping, and strangers closing in, I said, "God, send me some answers, please!"

My phone rang. A friend told me about Tim Heath, a mystic healer in Sedona, Arizona. I listened and agreed to meet him. In our first session, Tim told me I was a healer, that I was clairaudient, and that he had known me many lifetimes. I thought he was nuts. He laughed and told me he was not my teacher; he said my gift was more refined than his, and that he was here to tell me who I was. He said I had introduced him to the breath many lifetimes ago.

I could barely hear him because I thought he was full of New Age crap. I was judging him so harshly I could not even look at him, but then he showed me he knew exactly who I was. He looked at me with a sly grin and said, "It gets real intense around relationship, doesn't it?" He had me. I needed answers. My life was spinning out of control, what was happening to me? He seemed to have the answers and he said, "Let me show you this breathing meditation. It is called pranayama yoga. It is an ancient practice. You used it in India." I only vaguely remember the last part because I was so checked out, but he had me with the relationship thing. Not expecting much, I said, "Sure, I'll try it." He showed me what he called the 'two-stage breathing.'

At this point in my life, this 30-minute breathing session was the most powerful experience I ever had. I'd never felt energy vibrate and pulsate through my body so intensely. I thought I was levitating most of the time, my emotions moved freely. I realized much later that my spirit entered my body that first session, it merged with my heart, and it whetted my appetite for more. I went to meet Tim in Sedona a month later for a retreat (I talk about this whole experience in more detail in *The Reluctant Healer*).

Tim explained clairaudience to me; he said it was a gift in the throat chakra, a gift connected to hearing and speaking, as well as writing. He told me that I can hear the answer to people's questions before they ask them, and that I hear people's thoughts. I thought everybody heard these things. He laughed and said it was a rare gift to have it to the degree I had it. "A gift or curse," I wondered. He told me I would develop it and learn to use it positively and that right now I did not have the discipline to know how to. Even stranger were the perpetual goose bumps I would get when he said things that seemed to deeply resonate with my experience. My ears rang and popped, and Tim looked at me and said, "That's your clairaudience." And I hadn't said anything! He then told me that he had developed his hearing, too. He said, "It is pretty good now, but not where yours will be."

This was my first real conscious awareness of my spiritual energy, and that everything was connected into it, even the stuck feelings. I discovered that the stuck feelings were energy about to explode inside of me. The breath work allowed me to open the valve and release the pressure. I quickly connected the dots that these stuck sensations were physical, emotional, mental, and even spiritual. When the strongest ones released, I felt it on all of these levels. The spiritual was the last to make itself known, and it occurred after all the other levels had released, relaxed, and were at peace.

The journey with Tim, and more accurately the journey of the reluctant healer, had many twists and turns. For the two and a half years I knew him, I sent Tim all of the people who were coming to me for healing. Our time together was abruptly ended when he died in a car crash. Suddenly the people I had been sending him turned back to me for healing and I had to make a choice. Upon making the decision to move ahead as a healer, I left behind the role of the reluctant one. From there I had to begin the practice in earnest, taking the responsibility to learn and teach the healing information that I discuss in these two books. One of the biggest tasks was for me to become a teacher of the breathing meditation that had done so much for my own development.

Breath work was the tool for connecting me directly to my spirit. You may say, "What is the spirit? How did you know it was the spirit?" I knew it; I felt it in my heart, and I can assure you that, when you feel it, you will never forget it.

From the first breathing session the breath work connected me to my energy, and it was like returning home. I learned that when I did the breath work my mind would relax, my body would relax, and then my emotions would move or express. I would start to feel open in my body. The vibration of my energy would become electric; I could feel it pulsing through me everywhere. Then my mind would relax even more and open to the Universe, my heart would open and I would feel myself connect to everyone and everything. I would feel a specific heat, vibration, and energy that I learned to recognize as the personality of my spirit as it moved through my body. Sometimes it would enter my crown chakra through the top of my head, and sometimes directly into my heart. It was always memorable.

Gradually, I was able to develop the clairaudience in a way that worked for me. As I explain in the intuition section, most of this development happened as I did the healing work helping others. My spiritual development accelerated as I became less reluctant to do the healing work. The more I helped others, the faster my gift fine-tuned itself. It was natural and easy. Eventually I realized my intuition was the byproduct of all the development. I was suddenly tapped into a Universal awareness and consciousness just by opening myself up. The deeper I went into this experience, the more answers I found. Was this a gift I had used many lifetimes? It took me a while to ease into that one.

Finally, I gave myself over to be guided by my spirit, by the intensity of my clairaudience, and by my connection to the Universe. Nature was my biggest ally in all of this. If anything ever became too much, wildlife would get in my face and distract me back to a place of neutrality.

BREATH WORK

In the beginning, the breath work is the primary tool for you as it has been for me. The initial assessment I have seen with even the most gifted people is the need for development and discipline around understanding energy. You need to be able to interpret all the subtle shifts happening with your energy and connect them to the cause. As you do this there is a tremendous increase in awareness to the connections within, and outside of you. The breath is the fastest, cleanest, cheapest, and most effective way to do this. It is a meditation you can have results with from as little as seven minutes of breathing per day. Once you experience the effect you will likely do the meditation longer several times per week, especially if you are feeling stuck. I have written about the breath in many places, from my first book, to my blog, newsletters, and magazine articles. Many are on my website www.thereluchealer.com. Find them and read them for more info.

The breath is a powerful way to open up, clear stuck energy, and access your spirit. Literally, as you breathe, you are bringing life force energy into the body with increased oxygen flow. This oxygen moves from the lungs into the bloodstream and makes its way to the brain. We are not hyperventilating, because the breathing is slower and more controlled. The oxygen stimulates the hypothalamus gland in the brain and it releases endorphins that activate the other ductless glands, or chakras as they are more commonly known in yoga and spiritual work. The oxygen is important because it not only alkalizes (reduces acidity in the blood) the body, it also encourages the brain to relax. That in and of itself is priceless for us Westerners. Anything to get the brain to relax!

The more a person works with the breath, the faster their energy will open. The more a person feels their energy, the faster they will release blocks and heal. Who doesn't want that? Sure, the breath is confronting. It takes discipline to move through the biggest blocks, which have the most resistance stored in them. However, the more a person develops their energy and opens their heart, the faster they will heal and be able to start assisting others.

This does not mean everyone becomes a healer like me. They may open themselves up to expression and write their book, sing their music, teach others about love and find their purpose in life. The breath is the fuel to get the energy moving. Once it is doing so, it tends to peak at the moment the vibration crescendos into the same frequency as the soul. When this happens the soul merges with the physical body in the heart and you feel love and Universal Energy Flow in an unforgettable way. This is what most people are waiting for in their spiritual quest for healing and enlightenment.

To learn the two-stage pranayama breath I suggest finding a healer I have trained, buying a CD/MP3, downloading the free meditation, or finding me in person. You may be able to learn it from others, but I will only be able to speak from what I know and how I know someone has been trained.

Different from most breathing meditations, all of the breath in the beginning is taken in and out through the mouth and not the nose. Yes, it is more confronting and less comfortable, but it is worth the payoff. Your brain wants things to be comfortable, so it can stay in control. If the brain/ego stays in control, it will continue to create the same experiences you have been stuck with. You breathe through the mouth and the first breath is deep into the belly where most of your energy is stuck. Without exhaling, you inhale a second time high up into the chest. This brings the energy from the low belly up through the heart to the top of the lungs. You then exhale through the mouth and continue a steady rhythm.

This is powerful for many reasons; it causes you to feel deeply into your body and any place you are stuck from holding onto anger, fear, or sadness. The more awareness you can bring to this stuck energy, the more it can move. Also, the more it may want you to stop, or resist. You can get distracted early on, start yawning, or get dizzy. Continuing to breathe will clear the block, and sooner or later, it will move. **Where awareness goes, energy flows.** As you do this work and as

your spirit flows into you, you will find peace and contentment. It is like returning home.

WHAT THE BREATH DOES

*It amazes me time and time again about the response I get
from having people do the breathing meditation, and the rich
experiences they relate. I wonder why people resist a practice that they tell me does so much to open them up. I cannot
help but think why wouldn't they choose to do this meditation daily? Why do people fight to stay the same? It does not
make sense to me. And then I remember recently saying, "The
world would not necessarily be a better place if everyone was
like me." We need all types of people to provide the mirrors of
opportunity to reflect upon our human existence. If the world
was all white, it would be a struggle to see anything, if it
were all black it would be hard to distinguish anything. It
takes contrast to see. It takes contrast to create a picture. Nevertheless, I wonder, I wonder why…*

*Karma is an amazing teacher. The things that we come
in here needing to see, learn, and experience the most, are the
things we are most blind to. The key is teaching people how to
recognize karma, how to be a bloodhound and not give up the
hunt for what blocks them, as opposed to quitting at the first
whiff of their old familiar patterns. This is the time to become
vigilant with awareness. It amazes me that when the going
gets tough, people stop breathing, stop meditating, and stop
working. This is the time to work hardest!*

*I am finally realizing the depth of what the breath does
on the spiritual plane. It brings you front and center with
your karma. If you are a young soul and are getting around*

to living your life with purpose, there may not be any urgency in doing the work around your karma. You may feel like you have numerous lifetimes left for that. Why hurry? If you are an old soul, with many incarnations under your belt, you may feel a great urgency to pursue freedom in this lifetime, you may not wish to waste any more time feeling lost, confused, or distracted.

The old souls are being pushed the hardest right now. Being an old soul does not make you special, it just means this is your time for healing. You are in the batter's box, while the young souls are off fetching a beer and popcorn. They are kind of aware they are sitting in the bleachers at a ballgame, and are not quite sure why they are not out on the field. It is a different experience for each. Neither is better. The same with people living their life, very few are aware of their spiritual life purpose, very few are aware this reality could be happening simultaneously with their physical, emotional, and mental life experience. Honestly, I am most interested in things spiritual. The breath is the doorway to the spirit. It opens us up and takes us down the pathway of our spirit, and that's where the fun starts!

ESSENTIAL OIL BLENDS

In *The Reluctant Healer* I wrote about essential oils that I use to complement the breath work. The oils help the body, and specifically the chakras, balance and open to the breath. In the beginning I used single, unblended oils such as frankincense, lavender, peppermint, etc. In some sessions I may have used 15-20 of these oils. As I trained more and more people to do healing work, I decided to blend specific oils for each of the seven chakras that would be easy to use and apply. From the best distillers and of the highest quality, the blends are specific concoctions I have put together to help you heal.

Even though the oils have a wonderful fragrance, they are blended more for potent healing than aroma. You do not have to be a healer to benefit. Each of the blends has 4-7 oils in them and there is a synergistic effect from the combination. Each does what its name implies. For more info on the oils, or to order them, visit the products section of my website (www.thereluctanthealer.com). The essential oil blends I have created are called:

Grounding – This oil is used on the arches of the feet to ground the body and the first chakra to the earth. It works better placed on the feet because this is where grounding takes place. This oil was my first blend.

Sexual Healing – This oil is applied to the low belly and back to bring healing to the second chakra. It is a powerful blend of oils that is consistently used by people needing sexual healing.

Flow – This oil is used on the solar plexus (will center) and spine. It releases stuck energy out of the solar plexus, and clears fear out of the spine.

Open Heart – This oil is rubbed onto the heart chakra, or breastbone, right in the center of the chest. It has an amazing aroma and helps the heart to open.

Expression – Place this oil on the throat chakra to facilitate the clairaudient gift of intuitive hearing and speaking. It is excellent for anyone who is called to be a great communicator.

Foresight – This blend is used on the third eye, or center of eyebrows. It is designed to facilitate the gift of clairvoyance, as well as intuitive seeing. It is excellent for anyone who needs to see through illusion and gain clarity.

Ascension – Gently rub this oil on the crown chakra, at the top of your head, and also on the third eye. This is a multi-use oil. Originally I designed it to help connect you to the Universe, and to all that is. It works perfectly for this, in both the crown and/or the third eye. *

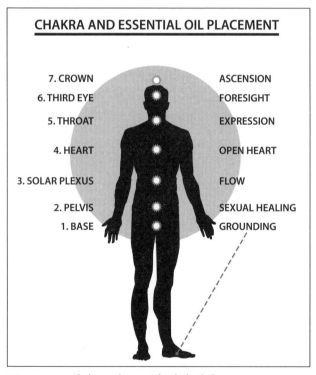

Diagram 12 – Chakra and Essential Oil Blend Placement

* Some people prefer not to have oil on the crown or in their hair, so I may use Ascension on the third eye and omit Foresight. Because Ascension can also be used on the third eye, it means the oil kits can be seven oils (with Foresight), or six oils (without Foresight). I prefer the complete kit, but 6 works just fine.

MEDITATION CD'S

1. **Breathing Meditation** – This breath work CD was my first and it is very helpful in guiding you with the breathing meditation. It is also available in Italian.

2. **Manifest** – My second CD helps you focus on manifesting abundance in your life. This can include material abundance, love, or a feeling of fullness and guidance around one's life purpose.

3. **Cleanse** – I created this third CD to help the breather on cleansing their space and themselves of any stuck, stagnant energy. The introduction teaches you how to set the cleansing in motion and many people who have been stuck have commented on the effectiveness of this CD.

4. **Sexual Healing** – My fourth CD is very powerful. So many people have sexual healing to do. This CD identifies and releases unwanted energies that are stuck in the second chakra.

5. **Spiritual Practice** – My fifth CD was a long time coming and it is the most versatile. It has four different-length meditations (7, 14, 21, and 28-minute). They are all good, and they offer more options for the breather based on the time they have available to breathe each day.

Free Meditation MP3 download - I have made this MP3 available to you as a sample of the breathing meditations. It has a brief introduction explaining how to do the breathing exercise and a seven-minute breathing meditation. Seven minutes is the bare minimum to experience this work. It is enough so that you will feel it, and I hope it introduces you to the breath in a good way!

Go to the Home Page of www.thereluctanthealer.com and sign up for the Free Meditation MP3 and Free Newsletter.

section five

GRATITUDE

Gratitude

Gratitude plays an important role in my life. I've told people it is one of the shortcuts to the heart, love and healing. It opens up the channels to the Universal Energy Flow. Gratitude is the great equalizer because it breaks down barriers and creates agreement to appreciate and get along with others. From the Universal perspective, gratitude complements the Power of Love like the rainbow does to our big blue sky. I am grateful to so many and I want to share my process of gratitude with you. So here goes…

LETTER TO RUBY

Ruby
To my daughter
My love for you will never falter
It extends beyond all the gifts I could ever give you
You warm my heart and tickle my soul
Your eyes reveal the depths of me
I seek comfort for you always

And I know our love will persevere through time and space
As it always has
As time moves forward know I will always be with you
Even when I am not
You will always be with me, even when I am not
Our souls will continue their dance through time and space

I am anticipating your birthday
It amazes me to witness the beautiful young lady you have become
As I look into the future I see your beauty expanding beyond my Imagination
If I can say one thing to you, always know you are loved
You are loved beyond belief
Your spirit is held in the highest esteem
Your gifts will be encouraged to grow
Trust them, trust yourself, and trust the Universe
Your life will contain elements of magic no matter where you go
Only you can open that treasure chest with your trust
It is never outside of you—anywhere
The spring from which it flows is deep inside your heart

If I can leave you with one gift
Trust your heart to show you the way
Love from this deep place will always keep you whole
Love from this deep place will always keep you happy
It is the most bountiful gift of all—love
You know this feeling
When you smile it radiates from inside of you
Trust this feeling let it grow

It can never be manufactured from outside of you
It flows from the well of creation, from the well of spirit
It is the elixir of life
Trust yourself to trust this love and your life will always be
full and happy

That is my eternal gift to you
That is your eternal gift to me
I love you forever and ever.

BUFFY

Any book I write about healing would not be complete if I did not refer and pay homage to my old friend, my dog Buffy. Below are some letters I have written to her since her passing.

10:45am, June 4th 2008
My friend, my ally, my buddy, my Buffer, my love, and my

joy; I say goodbye to you in this final moment of our journey together – at least in this body this lifetime for you. I adore you for your unwavering loyalty and friendship. My heart will never be the same without your physical presence near. The sadness for the loss of your companionship will forever leave me longing to re-connect with your sparkle and smile. You have been the friend who has taught me the most about fatherhood, and you prepared me for Ruby. I will always respect your stepping aside for my daughter to come front and center into my life. You have continually been so generous with your love and patience. You taught me how to care for another, and you taught me responsibility. I think about how much I have grown in our 18 1/2 years together, and my heart opens wide as I set you free to explore the realm of the spirit. Say "hi" to all of my friends on the other side. Visit them and rest your soul for this time. Do not stress, or worry about me. I will be okay. When it is time for you to travel back to me I will help you come through to this dimension. Just know that I will be holding a sacred space for you in the meantime. You will always be within my heart.

Kindly, your servant David

7:30am, July 4th, 2008
Buffy, it has been one month since your passing. I miss you every day. I grieve when I think of you, and I grieve without thinking of you. I miss you immensely. My life is not the same without you near. And yet I feel you near all of the time. When my heart opens to let your spirit run through me, I connect to your love and spirit as strong, if not stronger, than I ever did. I let you come to me, come through me, and guide me on my way. You always needed to be out front, now you can be out

front all of the time. I trust that you will come to me when the time is right. I am keeping my eyes open at all times. I feel your presence very strongly in Kitty. I feel your energy in her. For now I think it is okay to be working through her. It feels like you want to be back in a dog's body soon. A body where you can run and romp, smell, sniff, and go on mountain bike rides with me. Just like old times.

10:45am July 1st, 2009
Buffy, I feel you nearer and nearer, and I am ready now for your next embodiment. Come on in, I am ready. It has been one year since your passing and I am still holding on to your ashes. I will release them soon.

GRATITUDE ⸱ EXERCISE 31

Remember gratitude is a shortcut and this is one of the few times I will give you a shortcut.

1. If you only do one thing, practice gratitude daily and it will exercise your heart in a beautiful way.

2. How much do you have to be grateful for?

3. Start each day off with, "I am grateful for…"

You can do this while you are in the shower, looking in the mirror, making coffee, or on your way out the door. It will pay dividends. Give it a try, and keep it in your life. Teach it to others, then you will be exchanging with the practice of gratitude. I am grateful for you!

UNIVERSAL ENERGY FLOW

I have to give credit where much of my teaching and knowl-edge comes from. I have always thought of it as common sense, or horse sense as we call it on the farm, and I am so grateful for the connection to Universal Energy Flow that I was born with. I consider it a luxury to have grown up on a farm, and have my father and grandfather teach me about the Universal Energy Flow, Mother Nature, conservation, respect for the land and all that it provides. This foundation is a natural part of me.

My granddad, James Samuel Elliott, 1990, Fancy Farm, KY

My grandfather was always at home with the land. This particular day he was showing me his garden and telling me about the secrets of turnips. My granddaddy had this way with the earth and nature that I truly admired. I would watch him spill seed on the ground and it would seem like the next day we would be eating juicy cantaloupes, cucumbers, okra, tomatoes, peas, and butterbeans. I learned so much from him and my father. They both spent endless hours with me showing me the beauty of farming and how Mother Nature responds to love and exchange. I was a lucky boy.

Other important teachers in my life, include Native Elders, Miss Tu Moonwalker and Miss Lané Saan, as well as Miss Cynthia Knudsen, who have all helped deepen my understanding of the concept of the Universal Energy Flow. They have helped me understand even more about these energies and my connections to them. They have also encouraged me to slow down, to not take anything for granted, and to truly open myself to receive the blessings from the Universe.

I have become a better listener, writer, healer, father, and earth guardian as I have practiced gratitude. I understand now how being grateful is part of the Universe and the natural energy flow with it. It is truly a circle, a rainbow, the Northern lights, a desert landscape, a pine forest, waterfall, lava flow, coral reef, wildlife, the wind, water, fire, and the earth. The Universal Energy Flow is truly a unifying Power of Love permeating the Universe, and I have endless gratitude for it.

SACRED OFFERINGS

My Thoughts Are My Prayers And My Actions Are My Meditations. It really is as simple as that. I am accountable for all I think and do. My life is as sacred as I want to make it. The choice is up to me.

"Are you having any fun yet?" This was the question my friend Tim Heath would always ask me. Over time I learned to understand the reason for the question, and now I live to have fun, to enjoy this life for all it has to offer, and to ground it in all the love I can possibly imagine. The grace that flows though the choice to love and be in the moment exchanging an openhearted existence with the Universe attunes me to the oneness of all.

As part of my gratitude for the abundance the Universe provides me, I also use some physical items to make offerings with tobacco leaves, sage, corn, cedar and Piñon pine. It is a lot of Native American tradition and in part I choose to use them because they grow abundantly on my property in New Mexico. I am able to connect to these plants and harvest them with the intention to use them as offerings. As I like to say, "Once a farmer, always a farmer!" During the fall I may offer apples, pine nuts, cornhusks, tobacco stalks to name just a few others. The idea is to give back to the land and to honor the animals who are also inhabitants here.

The actual process I do is simple. When I arrive and when I leave my property for extended periods, I walk the property boundaries and sprinkle the ground with a mixture of tobacco, sage, corn, cedar and pine shavings. I have placed certain rocks in the four directions and I touch these stones, to give gratitude to the land, the trees, rocks, fence and gate for securing and protecting this sacred piece of property. It is really a simple walk and it is doubtful that someone who saw me would even be aware what I was doing. The outward display is not important, however the inward display is what is important for the Universe, this land, and me. The simple acknowledgments of gratitude, offerings, and love help us open to the Universal Energy Flow, which creates even greater peace and harmony here.

SACRED OFFERING ~ EXERCISE 32

There is no secret to this exercise. All it takes is a moment of conscious choice to have gratitude and to offer something in exchange for all the Universe provides you. It can be as simple as some flower petals, a homemade cookie, or some water offered to a plant or tree that brings you joy. It is about the moment of acknowledgment and exchanging love back to something that gives to you.

1. Pick something in your life that makes you happy —it can be your house, a person, pet, or even your car.

2. Decide on a really simple way to exchange with this person or thing. e.g. you may wash the windows on your house, give a person a back rub, brush your pet, or check the oil in your car. You may already do these things and the only adjustment you may need is awareness that you are giving gratitude to the other for the joy they bring to you. It is that simple.

TOBACCO

Tobacco is a plant that has been used for thousands of years as a sacred offering. With indigenous cultures, the smoke was typically offered up to the gods in the heavens.

Below is a beautiful story about tobacco:

> *Huron Indian myth has it that in ancient times, when the land was barren and the people were starving, the Great Spirit sent forth a woman to save humanity. As she traveled over the world, everywhere her right hand touched the soil, there grew potatoes. And everywhere her left hand touched the soil, there grew corn. And when the world was rich and fertile, she sat down and rested. When she arose, there grew tobacco . . .*

This myth is such a beautiful story and so appropriate with Great Spirit sending forth a woman to bring about the nurturance from potatoes and corn (Similar to the story of White Buffalo Calf Woman who brought the pipe and other sacred ceremonies to the Native peoples). Most importantly, when the world was rich and fertile she sat down and rested, similar to the seventh day in other spiritual teachings. In these moments of rest, satisfaction and gratitude, a plant is brought forth to offer up the prayers of gratitude to the Great Spirit. Forgive me for my interpretation, for I know it is probably missing many other analogies; nevertheless, this myth clearly states to me the importance of tobacco to the people who were working with it thousands of years before the Europeans.

Of course it did not take the rest of the world long to want to covet the powers of tobacco. In the coveting of anything, the true power will be twisted and lost. I am certain this is what happened to the purity of tobacco. Its essence got lost in the translation of commerce and consumption by the rest of the world. And here we are.

This analogy says so much. Could modern man be educated about the origins and powers of a plant such as tobacco? Would they even care? This is a perfect example of the status of the planet right now. It is an example of how our relationship with most things we are engaging with in our modern lives is missing true connection. It says everything to me about our relationship with Mother Earth and her resources. It says everything to me about how we interact with the environment; the earth and its oil and minerals; water and its oceans, rivers, lakes, springs, aquifers, and glaciers; air, soil, fire, plants, and the animals.

Does tobacco hold some key for us to make amends, to make prayers and offerings to Great Spirit? I know it is not within most people to connect to the Universe and pray the way indigenous people do; however, it could be a start for some.

When I pause and take a moment to pray, to make offerings, to connect to spirit, I step into an active exchange of love with the Universe that is key to everything for me. Tobacco helps bridge this connection from me to something much bigger, the Universal Energy Flow, and this exchange expands me to more love. I'm citing this example to get you to think of the ways you can have gratitude and what might be the offerings that help you connect to that.

For my mother it is her flowers, and her roses in particular. When she is in her yard working with her plants, she is at peace. Prayer time for her is when she is exchanging with

her roses, as well as the time she spends in Church. I am fine
with all the different ways she and everyone works to connect
to more love, whether that be through religion, other types of
spiritual practice, art, or anything that brings consciousness
to make offerings and connect to the Universe. I believe we
need more connection and gratitude wherever it comes from.
I recognize a commonality of man when we are peacefully
co-existing with one another and I see this commonality rep-
resented as love.

SAGE

Sage is another sacred plant I use and relate to. It speaks to
me like the tobacco plant does. Sage is an ally for me in the
healing work. It makes my job easier, and supports me in my
work with myself and others. Sage does this by helping clear
negative energy.

I love the smell of fresh sage, I love the smell of sage tea,
I love the smell of a sage leaf burning. Every time I engage
with sage I thank it for assisting me. I have a special relationship with a mother sage plant in the mountains. She has
spoken to me for close to twenty years now. She provides me
with the sage I use in the healing work, and in turn I bring
her water and tobacco as offerings. I thank her for her support and I have collected her seed for many years now. I have
given my word to reseed her if fire were to take her away. We
have a strong alliance.

ELK

While I am on the subject of gratitude, I am very grateful for
the spirit of Elk. It has been working with me for a few years

now. It is uncomfortable for me to talk about because I am being guided to hunt the elk for meat this fall.

At first I was appalled and said no. But it kept coming into my mind, my dreams, and physical reality; so I had to deal with it. New Mexican locals kept talking to me about elk hunting and the meat, then people started giving me the meat to eat. I kept hearing the 'voice' tell me that elk has some vital energy for me that I need at this time. I know this sounds strange, but I am sharing it with you just the way it is showing up for me.

My friend Robert mentioned that if I wanted to go elk hunting, we would have to put ourselves in for a lottery draw. I thought this could be my way out, it could head off the endeavor in case my imagination was making this up, right? Several locals said the lottery was a scam and that they had never been picked. I was notified my name was drawn the other day. I will be going on the elk hunt with Robert; we both get to take one elk. I am still uneasy about the whole thing. I have not shot an animal before, but the elk keeps telling me it will be okay. I think I can go through with the process, and I am being pushed to do so. I'll let you know what happens.

PIPE

I am also being instructed to get a pipe ready and to work more deeply with it, the tobacco, and the elk. There is much Native American spirit in my bones; my spirit knows these indigenous people as my own. I know this because I feel it; I resonate with their story. The pipe has been akin to a dowsing rod of clarity and information for me during the recent couple of years, especially since I began growing tobacco, and listening to the elk.

CREATIVITY

In some ways I am just getting started with my creativity, there is so much more! I have so much gratitude for my creativity expressed through writing because it gives me a chance to hear into my feelings and to think about them. It provides me an opportunity to feel my emotions in a new time and in a new way. Writing also gives me time to think about my thoughts and the way I want to put them together to express myself. Writing is a meditation around my ability as a communicator. It is a practice that requires discipline as well as commitment. It creates space for me to step back, contemplate, read and process my thoughts and feelings. I always say, "Writing is a cheap form of therapy."

As I said before, I am an artist; I live my life as an artist. All the work I do with people, nature and the planet I look at as art. Creativity is a shortcut to healing, spirit, and Universal Energy Flow. Creativity makes the artist Universally relatable and able to convey imagery in a unique way based on one's ability to love, be seen and heard. I am very grateful for all the creativity I have access to.

GRATITUDE AND OFFERING

EXERCISE 33

1. Record the ways you are practicing gratitude and offerings. Celebrate that practice with others.

2. Remember gratitude and offerings are a shortcut to the heart, love and healing. They open up the channels to the Universal Energy Flow.

Wrapping up the Healing Journey

Wrapping up the Healing Journey

Congratulations for getting to the end of this book! You have made a big commitment to yourself doing the exercises, meditations, and re-reading several sections. I am impressed. Like I said early on in the book I know this will be a chore, but don't you think you are worth it? Self-love and healing is the key to life. Keep this book handy, it will serve you for a long time to come. Remember, you are always worth the investment of learning how to love yourself. There is no other investment like it. The dividends are infinite. Life truly is an adventure and I have immense gratitude for your appetite for healing and in any way you share your experience with others.

I have started a nonprofit called the Creative Healing Arts Center and its vision statement sums up this book and where I am headed with my work.

CREATIVE HEALING (HEART) ARTS CENTER

Nonprofit Corporation Vision Statement

My vision for the *Creative Healing Arts Center* nonprofit corporation is that this center becomes an axis of 'good' for the planet. Positive healing, light, love-filled messages will spiral out of this center to people, to nature, to Mother Earth, and to the Universe. Ways that this intention will be demonstrated will be through education, wildlife rescue, and land and water conservation.

People will be taught how to heal themselves by using energy, creativity, and consciousness. As people balance and heal they will be educated to work with nature, and Mother Earth. Wildlife rescue will include hawk, owl, and hummingbird. Additionally, people will be taught how to garden and grow their own organic foods, and how to reclaim and conserve land, water, and natural resources.

This nonprofit corporation will be a spiritually based organization, but not limited to a specific religious belief. All will be welcome as long as they come in peace. Peaceful coexistence with all things will be a requirement for anyone who enters this organization and its property.

The philosophy this nonprofit will operate under is:

- We are all equal.

- We are all one.

- Love is the greatest force in the Universe.

- We accept a Higher Power.

- We all have access to this Higher Power to heal.

- We are all healers in some way.

Because of the high number of creative artists interested in this work, there will be a focus on spreading positive messages to be experienced by everyone through all medias. The

Creative Healing Arts Center will take responsibility to create harmony in the world. The overall energy of love, creation, respect, and gratitude will be aspired to at all times.

Nonprofit status allows us the financial means to get the corporation off the ground. It will be vital to accept tax deductible donations from those interested in contributing to this vision, as well as alliances and support from any like-minded governmental agencies/organizations.

Website: www.creativehealingartscenter.org

Once again I think of my friend Tim, all he predicted and his words to me twenty years ago. "David, are you having any fun yet?" I figure I am here to enjoy the ride. I love nature, the planet, animals and people. So, I might as well have as much fun as possible! You're welcome to travel along!

In the meantime I welcome you to correspond and let me know how this material is working for you. You are welcome to email me, david@thereluctanthealer.com, or comment on my blog http://blog.thereluctanthealer.com.

Keep up the good work, and I hope to meet, see, and hear from you at some point.

Aho mitakuye oyasin – For All My Relations
Namaste'
Peace
Amen!

LOVE, David

Acknowledgments

Mom, I acknowledge you for valiantly carrying on in your life without Dad at your side. I know it has been incredibly hard for you to adjust to life without your partner of fifty years, and I am proud of the strength you exhibit every day of your life. I am forever grateful for the work ethic both you and Dad provided me with. Thank you for all you have given me Mom! I love you, David

I send love and gratitude to you Dad in heaven. I know you are watching from above and I am sure you are having a good time up there. I am eternally grateful for your love, support, and example on how to be a good person in life. Thank you and I love you! David

I am very grateful and appreciative to all the people who have helped me complete this book, starting with Katrina Rivers and Corrie Borris, who have gone above and beyond the call of duty, giving endless hours of editing talent, expertise and dedication to this book and the healing work. I also wish to thank Gali Kronenberg for his skilled edits, insights, spiritual knowledge and big heart. I am overwhelmed with gratitude to Charlie Griak for his artistry and illustrative talent, and for all the other people including Simon and Kate Warwick Smith who helped me finish this book on HEALING. Also I thank my sister Julie for all of her love and support in this work, and my assistant Nisha for her love, support, and all that she holds down for me as I am traveling around.

Additionally, I would like to thank all of the many clients who have come to me and graced me with their love, trust, exchange, and appreciation. I thank all of the healers who have learned this work and are carrying it forward in the world. And if you have picked this book up and are working with it, I am very grateful for the exchange of awareness as you interact with this material. Thank you!

Lastly, I would like to thank all of the Universal Energy Flow, all the love, exchange, and support from the Universe. I am so appreciative of the magical creatures that guide me moment to moment in my life including the hawk, hummingbird, raven, crow, elk, dog, cat, and whale beings—to name a few. I am eternally grateful for all the beings of light including God, Jesus Christ, Archangels Gabriel, Uriel, Raphael, and Michael; Mother Mary, Quan Yin, Buddha, and Krishna. Also recognition to the beings of special intuition including Merlin, Tecumseh, Sweet Medicine, and my daughter Ruby. As well I honor the artists, writers, the Creative Healing Arts Center writer's group, and creative people everywhere! We are not alone! Let's Go!

Love, David

Appendix 1

FURTHER PONDERING FOR THE MIND

- Do we evolve because of our consciousness, or do we have consciousness because of evolution?

- We like to think consciousness is a human quality, but is it?

- What did the Universe have to do to ignite, to start to form and come together to create life?

- What suddenly started the energy moving?

- Was space always in existence?

- Is there such a thing as time, or a beginning, or even an end?

The possibilities of conjecture are endless, but the fascinating thing for me is how we seem to think the Universe revolves around us. Does it? It was here long before us, and I am certain it will continue long after our departure. However, as exceptionally bright sentient creatures, we do have endless possibilities to interpret life, the meaning of life, and the predictions of life. Here are even more questions to ponder in your free time.

- Is the human life span on Earth truly an experiment?

- Is the human life span in the Universe an even bigger experiment?

- How and why does the spirit exist?

- Why are we here?

- Are we excellent record keepers?

- Do we have exceptional possibilities to evolve through love?

- Could we play some role in the evolution of the earth, played out into the larger arena of our Milky Way galaxy, played out even farther to the ends of the Universe?

With this statement I am suggesting an exceptional importance to human existence, and I am moving way beyond anything individuated to an overall consciousness of us as humans. Truthfully I am speaking about the human potential for consciousness, which we certainly have not reached. Within this potential, is it going to take scenarios of possible extinction and devastation to rally humans to come together as one consciousness? Is it even remotely possible? How many would go down with the sinking ship to remain unconscious?

What will you choose to do with your time, energy, and emotions here this lifetime? I hope you become conscious about what you do. I am specifically focusing the work I do in the attempt to train people how to navigate their experience of life through their intuition. If you learn to develop your intuition in a pure way, then the guidance through the intuition can be honored and worked with. The byproduct of this is freedom from negative emotions! When negative emotions no longer control you, positive emotions become the notes, and intuition becomes the violin to play the music of your life. If you are led by your emotions in a reactive way then your intuition is propped up on a toothpick. It cannot be developed or trusted because you do not know who you are at the true essence point. You only know who you are based on how you are reacting to those around you. I have hope people can develop themselves with their intuition, so they can be neutral and clear in their choice of what actions to take with their lives.

Appendix 2

MEDITATION FOR YOU

Life in this Universe is an amazing adventure. Who really knows for sure about all the ways the Universe operates? Based on prior experience and collected data (wisdom), it would seem that there is some order and consistency. Some call this Natural Law. But then I wonder who keeps track of the amendments as we change and as the Universe changes. Is it being recorded somewhere, so that it can be acknowledged, verified, and referred to? Is there indeed a filing system called the Akashic Records?

The Akashic Records is a term used to describe a compendium of mystical knowledge encoded in a non-physical plane of existence. The concept originated in the theosophical movements of the 19th century, and remains prevalent in New Age discourse. These records are said to contain all knowledge of human experience and the history of the cosmos. They are metaphorically described as a library, and have also been referred to as: the cosmic mind, the Universal mind, the collective unconscious, and the 'Mind of God.'

It is said the records are constantly updated and that they can be accessed through astral projection. Some believe the Akashic Records make clairvoyance and psychic perception possible. According to believers, the Akasha are the library of all events and responses concerning consciousness in all realities. Every life form therefore contributes and has access to the Akashic Records. Any human can become a physical medium for accessing the records, and various techniques and spiritual disciplines (e.g. yoga, pranayama, meditation, prayer) can be employed to achieve the focused state of awareness necessary to access the Records. Just as conventional specialty libraries exist in research centers, believers describe the existence of various Akashic Records for the human, animal, plant, and mineral kingdoms that encompass all possible knowledge. Most writings refer to the Akashic Records in the realm of human experience, but adherents believe that all phenomenal experience as well as transcendental knowledge is encoded therein.

If indeed this recording system does exist, what does it all mean? Is there an order to the Universe? Is everything connected? Is anything random? What do you think?

I believe everything is connected and that nothing is random. One of the puzzling things to me has always been... who is driving the ship? Is there an overseer; is there one consciousness that holds it all together? Is that consciousness what religious followers refer to as God? Is there a multitude of consciousnesses, or are we all tapped into the same pool of awareness. The Universe is an amazing adventure for me, how about for you? If you have some of these same questions I have created one last meditation for you.

THE LAST MEDITATION ≠ YOU TELL ME

1. Lie down.

2. Get yourself as centered and clear as possible.

3. Do 10-15 minutes of the pranayama two-stage breath. Do not worry about having to remember all of these points, just read them a few times and they will be there.

4. When you feel your energy start to move very strongly through your nervous system and body—relax.

5. Let yourself vibrate, open your heart.

6. Let your crown chakra open; encourage your base chakra to ground into the earth. Feel yourself open up even more. If you find yourself in your head thinking, breathe for 5 more minutes.

7. Gently approach your brain and ask it to let go of control and allow your imagination to be free for 10 minutes. Promise to gift your brain later with some juicy stimulation—a nice book, computer game, or movie.

8. As your brain relaxes and you start to vibrate imagine your spirit entering your body through the crown, encourage your spirit to bless your hypothalamus and pineal glands (in the brain) with wonderfully nurturing Universal love. Bathe these glands in love! As the

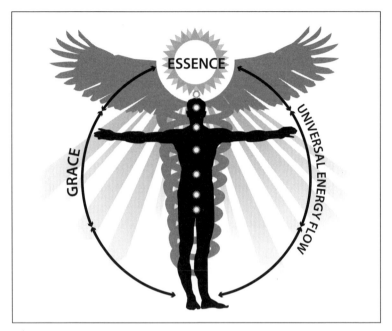

Diagram 13 – Essence 2

vibration increases, allow your imagination to connect to a spinning sunflower of light just above your
head, this sunflower is your essence. Allow your essence to flow into your crown and gently make its
way down into all of your chakras.

9. Ask your base chakra, the coccyx bone region, to gently connect down to Mother Earth. Ask permission
to gently grow roots down into the earth 5-10 feet,
moving like earthworms massaging the Mother as
you grow. Let these roots grow laterally as well as
vertically. Ask the Mother if you can send her love
and gratitude for her support. Gently release love and
support into her. In exchange the Mother will send

nurturance back into you. Let this energy flow in and up your chakras.

10. As you experience this connection, spirit flows in from above as from below. Let these energies come together in your heart. Let them mix and mingle.

11. When the energy flow starts to balance and settle, ask the Universe if it would be willing to exchange energy, information, and wisdom with you in exchange for your gifts. This might be nurturance of planet; development of your own consciousness in relation to the Universe; taking responsibility with your heightened awareness; or stepping into your awakening to help others.

12. Ask the Universe if it has a message or gift for you at this time. If you receive a big bundle of information, ask the Universe to interpret and clarify if needed.

13. Ask the Universe to show you your role at this time. Ask it to help you connect the dots around your life and purpose here on the planet now.

14. Ask the Universe if it has anything to teach, or show you about the age of awakening happening on the planet. How is humanity evolving, and where do we go from here?

15. Listen with your heart. Pay attention with your heart and let your mind stay calm. When you have received enough information, whether you see, hear, or feel it, notice your energy, notice your spirit. Acknowledge all the energies, thank your spirit, mind, imagina-

tion, intuition. Offer thanks to the Universe, Mother Earth, and all the positive energies that showed up to help you with this process. Thank your humor!

16. Once you have completed your process, start to come back, move slowly. Take out a notebook and write it all down, you may need it as a reference someday soon. Enjoy!

Once you have done this meditation let me know how it goes, and what you have learned. How does it all flow together for you? Are you connected to a larger consciousness of energy? Is this energy willing to communicate with you, to you and through you? If, yes, then maybe you are about to find your way in life, wouldn't that be a relief? Share this meditation with others. Go forth and have as much fun as possible!

Glossary

Spiritual words have many definitions and interpretations; therefore, in this glossary I will define how I am using them in this book. In most cases I will be coming from a Universal perspective, with 'the Universe' encompassing the various names used such as God, Creator, Divine, and Great Spirit. My own spiritual practices and work draw on many religions, philosophies, and cultures and I have been deeply influenced by people from these various traditions.

Aggressive – Violent, forceful, destructive, belligerent.

Aggressive consumerism – Destructive materialistic attitude.

Aho Mitakuye Oyasin – A Native American, Lakota Sioux, term meaning 'for all my relations.' I have been taught to use this term with utmost respect upon entering and leaving a sacred place such as a sweat lodge, medicine wheel or a circle. Oftentimes the shortened form 'Aho' is used to signify agreement.

Akashic Records - A term used to describe a compilation of mystical knowledge encoded in a non-physical plane of existence. These records are described to contain all knowledge of human experience and the history of the cosmos. They are metaphorically described as a library. Other terms commonly used to describe them include a 'universal computer' and the 'Mind of God.' The Akasha is a Sanskrit term for 'sky' or 'air.'

Alliance – An agreement between two or more parties for a common purpose—e.g. an alliance between countries would be an agreement to work together for peace, or an alliance with an animal in the wild would be to develop an agreement to work together to help each other. An example with a hummingbird alliance could be to plant some flowers they love or install a feeder for them to enjoy in exchange for them helping you with your intuition. In this spiritual agreement with the hummingbird you can ask them if they would be willing to help you develop your intuition by flying close by your face when the Universe is sending you information.

Amen - Hebrew for "so be it," signifying an affirmation, commonly used at the close of a Jewish or Christian prayer or hymn.

Chakra – A Sanskrit term for 'wheel,' 'disk,' or 'turning.' In Indian medicine energy, Hinduism, and other Eastern philosophies it refers to the seven energy centers of spiritual power in the body which are the same as the ductless glands associated with Western medicine.

Clairaudience – Intuitive hearing and speaking, located in the throat chakra, corresponds to the throat and thyroid gland. A 'gift of prophecy.'

Clairsentience – Intuitive knowing, located in the heart chakra, corresponds to the heart and thymus gland. A 'gift of knowing.'

Clairvoyance – Intuitive seeing, located in the third-eye chakra, corresponds to eyes and the pineal gland. A 'gift of vision.'

Consumerism – A belief in the benefits of consumption, or a materialistic attitude.

Divine – Heavenly, Godly, celestial; of the Universe.

Ego – Personality, self, self-image; inflated opinion of oneself.

Entity - A negative thought form, or energy that disguises itself as the person or part of their personality. A parasite that feeds off the energy of a host, be it a person, animal, or plant.

Essence – Soul, spirit, core, identifying nature. I use the term synonymously with the word soul.

Exchange – The flow of consciousness given and received as energy, respect, value, appreciation, and love. It can also refer to goods, services and money.

Faith – Belief or trust in the Universe. Faith is the outcome of grounding self-love as one's reality.

God – Supreme Being, creator, the center and focus of religious faith, a holy being or ultimate reality to whom worship and prayer are addressed. I use the term Universe synonymously with the word God.

Grace - The Universal Energy Flow as it flows back to us in a form we can recognize such as a vibration, temperature, or tone of energy. This description is slightly different from the religious context. In this context, grace is the byproduct created from the agreement to love and exchange.

Intuition – Instinctive knowledge not based on intellect or reason. A sixth-sense, or insight. Intuition is an ability that can be developed.

Karma – A Sanskrit term that means 'action' or 'deed.' This concept in Indian philosophy refers to the sum total of one's actions—good and bad. These actions are attached to the soul as it transmigrates. Each new body (and each event experienced by that body) is determined by previous karma. Colloquial: What goes around, comes around. What you sow, you too shall reap. Universal Law of Cause and Effect.

Love – An energy of the heart and soul. It expands and uplifts you when felt and expressed. It is the human emotion people most desire. When you feel love within, it spirals outward and connects you to all existence through the opening of the heart.

Money - Any medium of exchange that is widely accepted in payment for goods and services and in settlement of debts. Money also serves as a standard of value, worth, or flow of resources.

Namaste' – A Sanskrit term meaning 'to bow.' This salutation from India is often accompanied with a gesture made with the hands held at chest height with both palms pressed together. Used as a greeting or farewell, it conveys the meaning, 'Bowing to you. The divinity in me recognizes the divinity within you.'

Natural Law – Considered to be an ideal to which humanity aspires, not the way human beings usually act. Assumed to be the permanent characteristics of human nature, that can serve as a standard for evaluating conduct and civil laws.

Negative Thought Forms – Indicative of 'no self-love,' parasitic energies that feed off of one's energy, and in the worst cases can cause illness. This kind of negativity may have been a comment someone made to you as a kid such as: "You're fat. You're stupid. You're ugly." Such words can stay stuck in your mind and body, along with the negative energy associated with them as negative thought forms if not healed on the spiritual level.

Parasite - Organism that lives in or on a second organism, known as a host. Parasites usually cause the host harm. In healing it is viewed more in energetic terms, as a negative energy that lives in your energy field and/or body and causes harm by feeding off of you (e.g. entity, negative energy, negative thought form).

Physical sexual abuse – When someone is raped, molested, or experiences unwanted physical contact that is sexual in nature.

Pranayama Breathing Meditation – A Sanskrit term from prana - breath, and yama – restraint. An ancient breathing technique from India that involves breathing in and out through the mouth to activate the internal vital energy flow. This meditation is one of the foundational tools in David Elliott's healing work. Can be downloaded free off of www.thereluctanthealer.com.

Predator – A person who specializes in taking other people's energy, especially through sexual energy. They are masterful at creating a connection that immediately feels safe, intimate, and trustworthy. They have hypnotic abilities and are able to psychically seduce an adult or child into thinking sexual energy is love.

Psychic – Spiritual, telepathic, supernatural, intuitive, extrasensory; not always of the light, can be positive or negative. In the positive sense it is a spiritual condition based in love, in its negative condition it is based in fear or fantasy.

Psychic sexual abuse – When someone is sexually abused on an energetic level and there is no physical contact; generally this happens in the higher, more spiritual realms because it is disguised as love.

Sanskrit - The ancient sacred language of India. Each Sanskrit letter is said to be imbued with its own color, sound and power. Sanskrit terms I use include akashic, chakra, karma, kundalini, namasté, and pranayama.

Seduction – The act of luring somebody into sex, leading them astray, and abusing them by doing this against their will, or conscious choice.

Sensitive - (noun) A psychic person, who is acutely perceptive.

Sexual abuse – Abusing someone by luring him or her into an exchange of sexual energy without their full awareness, or against their will. This abuse can happen physically, emotionally, mentally, spiritually, and psychically.

Sexual abuse energy – The energy that is passed into the victim. This energy leaves an imprint that acts as an entity restimulating the person time and time again on all levels, moving as a sexual energy, both consciously and unconsciously.

Sexual energy – The energy that moves through the sexual regions of the body (2nd chakra), which can be expressed in positive as well as negative ways.

Soul - In many religions and philosophies it is considered to be the immaterial element that together with the material body makes up what it is to be human. In this work I use the word soul synonymously with the word essence.

Spirit – Called soul in many religions. I refer to it in this work as the expression of the soul, the personality of the soul; the way it moves and grabs your attention. For instance, a particular vibration, the flow of fire and heat as energy, goose bumps, or movement of electricity through your nervous system are all ways one's soul or essence expresses itself as spirit.

Spiritual – Of the soul; sacred, divine, mystical, holy, saintly, the light.

Spiritual Karma – The primary lesson your soul has been working on with its journey to healing.

Spiritual Life Purpose – The point in life where the spirit gives direction on the desired expression and activity to bring healing to the individual on their deepest life levels. When a person is 'On Purpose,' his or her work and everything one does 'clicks' and provides the greatest satisfaction in daily life.

Stubborn – Inflexible, obstinate, persistent, 'pigheaded.'

Suppression - Repression, hushed-up, control, or forceful prevention.

Universe – An all-encompassing energy including the various names of God such as Creator, Divine, or Great Spirit.

Universal Energy Flow - The natural flow of energy exemplified in the earth, sun, moon, sky, stars, waterfalls, oceans, rivers, springs, deserts, glaciers, air, wind, storms, forests, trees, jungles, wildlife, and rainbows. Humans can access the Universal Energy Flow when they are in a place of love. It can flow into them and be exchanged with.

Vibration – An electrical frequency or the way the spirit moves through the body. This can take the form of shaking, trembling, pulsation or force.

Victim – Injured party, prey, helpless person. Most people display strong compassion for a victim.

Written Exercise Work Summary

Written Exercise Work Summary

I recommend you purchase a journal and work on all of the exercises to document your journey."

EXERCISE 1 ⋰ LOVE

1. Write down all the ways you love yourself. If you have difficulty doing this exercise then we have found the key to your healing! Risk Loving Yourself!

2. Work at this until it is easy and something you do every-day. It may seem cliché but it is vitally important to your healing on all levels - physically, emotionally, mentally, and spiritually.

EXERCISE 2 ≠ EXCHANGE

1. Write down your definition for exchange.

2. Write down every relationship where you do not feel appreciated and valued in your life.

3. Write down the areas where you feel abundantly appreciated, and valued.

4. Compare the two - appreciated to unappreciated.

5. Check in with yourself right now, do you live in deficit around exchange? Or do you live with abundance? How do you feel in this moment—uplifted, or deflated? Your feeling will tell you where you stand with exchange.

EXERCISE 3 ≠ NATURE

1. Write about one of your most magical experiences in nature.

2. What happened?

3. Reflect back to what was going on with you just before nature came into the picture.

4. Was your heart open? Was love flowing through you?

5. Was your heart closed? Did nature help it open?

6. What happened to you after your interaction with nature?

7. Did you feel excited, inspired, opened up?

8. Connect the dots – love, exchange, Universal Energy Flow, nature, grace, and you.

9. If you felt any step was missing in the experience, claim it now.

10. Call the experience back using your memory. Open to love and exchange with nature; receive the Universal Energy Flow and allow the grace to flow to you.

11. Do something good with it.

EXERCISE 4 – SELF-LOVE AS A CIRCLE

Meditate on the Love & Exchange Diagram (p. 45) depicting the completed circle of self-love and Universal Energy Flow.

EXERCISE 5 – DISCIPLINE

A six-month prescription for you:

1. Read this book and do all of the exercises – take your time with it!

2. Read The Reluctant Healer and do all of the exercises. People have reported miraculous healings just doing the exercises!

3. Learn the pranayama breathing meditation and practice daily, a minimum of seven-minutes per day. This will complement any spiritual practice you are already doing. You can download a free meditation MP3 on the Home Page of my website www.thereluctanthealer.com.

4. If you miss a day, jump back in the next. You will love this simple seven-minute practice and will feel lighter and more joyful immediately.

5. Let me know how your progress goes.

6. Discipline is key!

EXERCISE 6 ≠ EXTREME

1. Write about the ways you feel like something is wrong with you.

2. Do advertisers have free access to your wallet by convincing you that your life could be a lot better if you bought their product?

3. What ways are you seducible because of being extreme?

EXERCISE 7 – AGGRESSIVE CONSUMERISM

1. Write down the areas where you know you have aggressive consumer energy (e.g. driving; being first in line anywhere; getting a parking spot at Wal-Mart; when you are hungry; when you are frustrated with electronics; over food and water when there is an emergency; around people who are less intelligent than you think you are, etc.). Make your list.

2. Write about the ways you feel justified to be the way you are because most everyone else is the same way.

EXERCISE 8 – AGGRESSIVE CONSUMER MEDITATION

1. Do the free breathing meditation mentioned earlier (p. 48), and set an intention to 'heal the aggression inside.'

2. As you start to tingle and vibrate, gently ask your mind to relax, ask your heart to open, and ask your spirit to guide you.

3. Ask your spirit to show you that you are safe and abundant.

4. Let the little child inside your heart feel safe and feel your love. Relax and enjoy the peace!

5. Take your time and exchange with the Universal Energy Flow.

6. Come back when you are ready.

7. Write down anything you experienced and what your spirit brought to you about your healing.

EXERCISE 9 ≠ ADDICTION

1. Write down the areas where there is addiction in your life (Alcohol, sex, sugar, nicotine, caffeine, drugs, TV, money, Internet, clothes, caretaking, control, stress, relationship, love, etc.).

2. In each area try to answer what you are seeking. What are your deepest thoughts around these addictions? Do your best to get to the bottom of each one.

3. What did you find out? Does it all come down to feeling like you are not going to be loved? That love will leave you? Are you angry about not being loved?

EXERCISE 10 ≠ EGO

1. Write about one relationship in your life when you felt the greatest addiction in all of your behaviors.

2. What were you looking for in this relationship? What was your ego looking for?

3. What kept you in it?

4. Are you still looking for what you thought you were going to get?

5. Was your addictive behavior due to you, the other person, or both?

EXERCISE 11 – BEING STUBBORN

1. Just check in with two people – Mom and Dad.

2. Write down anything you have to forgive, forget, let go of, and heal with them. Then do it.

3. If you cannot do this, then you are holding them accountable for something you need to deal with inside of you. More than likely there is stubbornness in this position. Let it go. When you set them free with love it will open up the next layer of intimate relationships around you, or waiting to come around you. It is time.

EXERCISE 12 – REVISITING EXCHANGE

If you have felt any place inside of you where you are:

Extreme

Aggressive

Addicted

Driven by ego

Stubborn

go back and review exchange.

EXERCISE 13 – MORE LOVE

1. Write about your concept or understanding about love. What does it feel like? Can you trust it?

2. How much of it is defined by what your parents showed you?

3. Do you know you need to expand your trust about what love really is?

4. Does the idea of loving yourself still confuse, frustrate, or elude you?

EXERCISE 14 – SHARING LOVE

1. Write down the ways you love yourself more since starting this book.

2. Share this with someone.

EXERCISE 15 = INTUITION

1. Develop a relationship with the pranayama breath work mentioned throughout the book. It is a fundamental tool in this work (see p. 48).

2. Develop your connection to your soul through the experience with the breath. Start to make notes of how the Universe communicates to you through your energy (e.g. I tingle and vibrate around my mouth, my hands get hot, I release stuck emotions, etc.). This is the key to developing your intuition.

3. Do you already have some guides and alliances that help you with your intuition? Try to list everything that comes to you in conjunction with your intuition. Put down everything you have memory of, and everything you are experiencing doing the breath work.

4. Take another sheet of paper and start to connect the dots, try to track your intuition in the general way that it communicates to you (e.g. truth, goose bumps, hawks, wind, heat, hummingbirds, warm fuzzy feeling in the heart—love, an awareness of Universal Energy Flow, the response of animals).

EXERCISE 16 – INTUITION – PART 2

Start to work with your awareness to develop these skills.

1. Every time you think of someone ask yourself, "Is this my thought or theirs? Am I generating it? Or are they?" If they keep 'randomly' popping into your mind it is usually their thoughts. You have to be clear here! You may not always know at first but be easy about it. If you engage with this your intuition will grow.

2. If it is your thought/energy ask yourself, "What do I want from them?" And proceed from there. You have to deal with you and take responsibility for your thoughts and feelings. Clean them up when necessary.

3. If it is their thought/energy ask yourself, "Does this feel like love? Does it lift me up? Is the vibration expansive?"

4. If it feels like love you can let it in and send love back. This is a circle. It will energize you and make you happy. This adds energy to the Universe and brings grace flowing back to you.

5. If it does not feel like love this is where the work and boundary development comes in. This is where clarity with your intuition is imperative! This is where you say "No!" to the thought/energy. Not welcome. You do not have to go to war. You can be gentle, but you must be firm. Most people do not expect to be handled on the psychic spiritual/plane. Most are not even conscious that their thoughts and feelings can be felt on this level.

6. When you say an energetic 'no' notice how many more times you have to say it. This will teach you how much work you have to do to strengthen your boundaries, and it will teach you about the energies you have aligned with to learn your lessons.

7. When one 'no' consistently handles these situations you will have reached a place of awareness where you can start to deal with your essence and true purpose in life. In other words the channels will be open enough, and you will be in touch with your intuition to be guided to remember who you are. From there it becomes a treasure hunt following spirit and its divine plan for your existence. Hallelujah! This is what most of us are searching for.

EXERCISE 17 ⁊ CREATIVITY

1. Write down the types of creativity you are sitting on, doubting, suppressing or resisting within. If you are frustrated, depressed or in a negative relationship in any aspect of your life then you are squelching your expression. The exchange between you and the Universe is off. It is time to love yourself, exchange with the Universe and set your creativity free.

2. Pick an art form—writing, singing, painting or dance—and unleash your creative expression with it. Exchange with your creativity, love it, embrace it! Use it to set your-

self free. When you become excited about your life because of your creative expression everything magically falls into place.

3. Make a commitment to express your creativity on a consistent basis. As you do this your confidence will grow. Take risks to express yourself. Give birth. Let yourself become excited and play! Dare to experiment.

EXERCISE 18 – CREATIVITY ⁄ MEDITATION

If you have a recorder, record this next section and use it in a meditation. I suggest doing ten minutes of the pranayama breathing and as you start to open and vibrate play this message that came through the 'voice' that guides me. There is an energy you can access through these words. I feel the energy when it comes through and I relay the message to you.

Who are you? Why are you here in this body this lifetime? Are you here to play the game or are you here to watch the game? If you know there is more to life than what you have been experiencing, if you have always felt this – then it is time to wake up. As I mentioned earlier it may be easier to remain asleep. At first it will be confronting to see, hear, and feel through the illusion that most humans live by, nevertheless, if you are able to hear this message it is meant for you. Most will pass it by; such is existence here on the true mother ship, Mother Earth.

If you can hear the message, and you have accumulated a wealth of training, knowledge, and information to share, it is time for you to awaken to your purpose. You are a messenger for the higher dimensional beings that work through the physical realms here on Earth. These beings have an allegiance to humans that is not based on our prior actions, but based more on our innate potential to love and be loved.

The Power of Love is vast beyond measure. It is beyond science and beyond intellect. It is a power that ignites the human spirit, and flows as light connecting us to all things – as One. We have underachieved with our potential to love and be connected to all things. We have isolated ourselves as 'the one, the superior, the dominant' power, disconnecting ourselves from all of the things that give us existence and life: namely the Earth, sun, stars, moon, sky, water, air, fire, nature – the Universal Energy Flow! We have been seduced by the Love of Power, which gets us nowhere.

The higher dimensional beings, call them God, angels, deities, spirits, masters, or light are choosing to get our attention now. They are calling forth the contracts signed long ago; for many the time of amnesia is over. If you know you are a messenger with a message to deliver, you will have to be the conduit for it soon, otherwise your contract will be taken over by another who will deliver the message, leaving you with a familiar empty feeling. If you know this feeling and you do not like it—get creating now! As you birth the message, those meant to engage with it will find it. Do not worry about the logistics. The higher energies will be your representative, your agent, your curator, your publisher and teammate. Let's go!

EXERCISE 19 – CREATIVITY – GETTING STARTED!

1. Take a big risk; tell your best friend you are going to start a creative project you have been waiting to do your whole life. For some of you it might be to write your book, for others it may be to buy a guitar and start taking lessons, for another it may be to work with watercolors, or for someone else it might be to simply write a poem. Let your heart guide you in taking this risk, it is not about your mind.

2. Share your risk with a family member.

3. Tell a complete stranger: "Got a new guitar today!" "I'm going to paint." "I'm writing poetry."

EXERCISE 20 – FINDING TRUTH INSIDE MEDITATION

If you are concerned with the world picture, the financial times, politics, environment, war, as well as peace, family and raising kids, then you benefit by cultivating your intuition to the point where it can be your inner compass:

1. Lie down.

2. Do the breathing meditation, or another meditation you like to get yourself to an open, neutral place (refer to p. 48).

3. When you are vibrating, ask your intuition to guide and work with you.

4. Pick one topic you would like guidance on (e.g. environment, family issue, relationship, politics, etc.).

5. Ask your intuition to show you the truth about the topic you chose. Let it come to you, you may see it, hear it, or feel it. Notice the sensation and the experience that comes to you. Relax and enjoy the truth.

EXERCISE 21 – SEXUAL ABUSE

1. What is your definition of sexual abuse?

2. What do you first think of at the mention of sexual abuse?

3. What is your story around sexual abuse energy?

4. What stage are you at in the healing of this abuse?

5. Do you believe you can heal it?

EXERCISE 22 – SEXUAL HISTORY

1. When was your first memory of sexual energy?

2. How old were you?

3. Who was connected to that memory?

4. Can you remember what happened?

5. How did it feel?

6. Did anything physical occur?

7. Was anything said, or expressed?

8. Was sexual energy disguised as love in any way?

9. How long did this situation persist?

10. Do you feel you were seduced?

11. Did you ever do this same thing to someone else? Even
    as a fantasy?

12. How do you feel about that?

13. Have these energies controlled you in any way?

14. Have these energies caused you to not trust the Power of Love?

15. Have these experiences tried to dominate your reality of life?

16. Do these energies make you sick?

17. Are you angry with these energies for controlling you?

18. Are you ticklish and extra sensitive around your pelvis and hips?

19. Has sexual abuse been in your family for many generations?

20. Are you ready to bring healing to your lineage?

21. Are you ready to experience the truth about love, healing, and exchange of Universal Energy Flow, which is free and clear of sexual abuse energy?

EXERCISE 23 ⋆ CANCER

Do you have cancer?

Have you had cancer in your life?

Do you worry about getting cancer?

If cancer is in your space (physically, mentally, or genetically), take the time to love yourself as deeply as possible.

1. Give the information in this book a try.

2. Commit to the discipline of daily breath work.

3. Let go of all upset.

4. Answer the wakeup call. What do you have to change in your life?

5. Do it now.

Choose love and life, and exchange with the Universe. If you love enough you can heal anything!

EXERCISE 24 — MARRIAGE AND DIVORCE

1. Have you been through a divorce, or a painful breakup?

2. What scars has it left you to heal before you open yourself to a new relationship?

3. Is some part of you waiting to be healed spiritually before you blindly leap into another's arms with the hope they are going to be the 'one?'

4. Do you have to love you first?

EXERCISE 25 — MARRIAGE AND DIVORCE

1. Has divorce, or a nasty breakup created a place where energy feels stuck inside of you, your family, children or pets that is waiting to be healed?

2. Is it time for a healing? Or are you waiting for your ex to be the one who initiates the healing, or say they are sorry?

3. How long do you intend to wait?

4. Does the power to forgive and move on reside in someone else, or inside of you?

EXERCISE 26 — INTIMATE RELATIONSHIPS — IMAGINATION

1. Imagine your perfect partner. What does he or she look like? How do they walk, talk, smile, play, etc.? What do you feel like as you envision the two of you together? Give yourself permission to go all out with this exercise. Dream it! Spend as much time on it as you desire. Is this partner the one you have been waiting for?

2. Look inside yourself now and see if you can imagine this person. Allow them to be real. This is not a fantasy. If you can imagine it, the process has begun, and it is real because it has happened inside of you.

3. Your partner is you. Accept it, make peace with it, and let yourself be filled with love. Let the birds sing around you. Let the Universal Energy Flow through you, to you, and back out. Grace accumulates and as the Universal Energy Flows out of you in a complete circle of expression, guess what happens? You manifest the love you are seeking internally and externally. Completion!

EXERCISE 27 – LEADERSHIP ROLES

1. Which position do you feel you occupy the most – leader or follower?

2. How do you fare in either? Are you needy, difficult or rebellious as a follower? Are you stiff, controlling, and domineering as a leader?

3. Are you able to maintain clear boundaries with people and not be a tyrant?

4. How do you lead, and play the various roles required of you to be an effective teacher and connect with others in a meaningful way?

5. How do you allow the Universe to be teaching you at the same time you are working with the people who are coming to you?

EXERCISE 28 – ROLE AS A FOLLOWER

- How do you show up in your role as a follower?

- Do you project lots of energy (love, needs, judgments) towards the leader?

- Do you rebel?

- Do you expect a leader to carry your pain?

- Do you expect the leader to take on your drama because of the way you are exchanging with them?

- Do you always work to get close to the leader in some way?

- Are you the teacher's pet?

- Are you the leader's pain in the behind?

- Are you needy with this person?

- Do you respect their private time?

- Do you work to prove yourself invaluable to them?

- Do you feel more comfortable if you can create their reliance on you?

- Do you work to create an intimate flow of energy from them?

- Do you always put the leader in a position to be hurting your feelings?

- Specifically what is familiar about the way you act with all of the authority figures in your life?

- Do you use your relationship with the leader to work out your issues regarding your worth and self-esteem?

- Are you hungry for the leader's love and approval?

- Do you compete for their attention?

- Do you set up romantic scenarios in your mind?

- Do you try to seduce the leader?

- Do you create karma with these people?

- Do you create ways to pull on the leader's energy at times when they are most vulnerable?

- Do you look to find fault with the leader, so you can have your way out when things get tough?

EXERCISE 29 – ROLE AS A LEADER

- How do you show up as a leader?

- Do you project lots of energy towards people who look to you for leadership?

- What are your expectations from students?

- Do you exhibit a lack of patience towards them when they are needy?

- Do you get sloppy with your boundaries?

- Do you allow yourself to develop romantic feelings and/ or situations with your students?

- Are you clear about the roles you play with your students?

- Do you seek out favorites?

- Do you allow certain students to overstep boundaries with you because they are 'special?'

- Do you allow yourself to become put off by certain people because of some quality, trait, or behavior?

- Are you confident in your role as the leader?

• Are you confident in your role as an authority figure?

EXERCISE 30 – MONEY

1. Write about your relationship with money. Take as long as you need.

2. Write about any similarities with your views on money and those of your family.

3. Do you feel like there is not enough money?

4. Do you feel abundant no matter how much money you have?

5. Does money own you?

6. Are you willing to trust money to flow to, around, and through you?

7. Are you open to money?

EXERCISE 31 ≈ GRATITUDE

1. If you only do one thing, practice gratitude daily and it will exercise your heart in a beautiful way.

2. How much do you have to be grateful for?

3. Start each day off with, "I am grateful for…"

You can do this while you are in the shower, looking in the mirror, making coffee, or on your way out the door. It will pay dividends. Give it a try, and keep it in your life. Teach it to others, then you will be exchanging with the practice of gratitude. I am grateful for you!

EXERCISE 32 ⚡ SACRED OFFERING

There is no secret to this exercise. All it takes is a moment of conscious choice to have gratitude and to offer something in exchange for all the Universe provides you. It can be as simple as some flower petals, a homemade cookie, or some water offered to a plant or tree that brings you joy. It is about the moment of acknowledgment and exchanging love back to something that gives to you.

1. Pick something in your life that makes you happy – it can be your house, a person, pet, or even your car.

2. Decide on a really simple way to exchange with this person or thing. e.g. you may wash the windows on your house, give a person a back rub, brush your pet, or check the oil in your car. You may already do these things and the only adjustment you may need is awareness that you are giving gratitude to the other for the joy they bring to you. It is that simple.

EXERCISE 33 ≈ GRATITUDE AND OFFERING

1. Record the ways you are practicing gratitude and offerings. Celebrate that practice with others.

2. Remember gratitude and offerings are a shortcut to the heart, love and healing. They open up the channels to the Universal Energy Flow.

Index

Index

"Close the Work"

NOTES

NOTES

NOTES

NOTES

NOTES

NOTES

NOTES